MAUPASSANT AND A CIGAR
AN INTIMATE BIOGRAPHY OF
PUDUMAIPITHAN

Mission Statement

This is an initiative of the TNTB & ESC under the aegis of one of the announcements for the year 2023-24 by the Honourable Minister for School Education Thiru Anbil Mahesh Poyyamozhi, titled the Translation of Rare and Nationalized Literary Tamil Works into English. These ventures are to be undertaken as either independent or joint publications with collaborating English language publishers.

Members, Academic Advisory Committee (Translation)

Dr R Balakrishnan, IAS, Researcher & Writer

Thiru S Ramakrishnan, Writer

Thiru S. Madasamy, Educationist

Project Execution Team

Thiru. Dindigul I. Leoni, Chairperson, TNTB&ESC

Dr. P Sankar, IAS, Managing Director, TNTB&ESC

Dr. M. Kuppusamy, Member Secretary, TNTB&ESC

Dr. T.S. Saravanan, Joint Director (Translations), TNTB&ESC

Dr. P. Saravanan, Assistant Director (Publications), TNTB&ESC

Thiru. M. Appanasamy, Consultant, TNTB&ESC

Tmt. Mini Krishnan, Co-ordinating Editor, TNTB&ESC

MAUPASSANT AND A CIGAR
AN INTIMATE BIOGRAPHY OF PUDUMAIPITHAN

THO MU SI RAGUNATHAN

TRANSLATED FROM THE TAMIL ORIGINAL BY

PEER MOHAMED AZEES

This book is being published under the Translation initiative of the Tamil Nadu Textbook and Educational Services Corporation

NIYOGI BOOKS

This book is being published under the Translation initiative of the Tamil Nadu Textbook and Educational Services Corporation

Published by
NIYOGI BOOKS
Block D, Building No. 77,
Okhla Industrial Area, Phase-I,
New Delhi-110 020, INDIA
Tel: 91-11-26816301, 26818960
Email: niyogibooks@gmail.com
Website: www.niyogibooksindia.com

Editor: Amrita Chakraborti
Design: Shashi Bhushan Prasad

ISBN: 978-81-19626-77-9
Publication: 2024

Disclaimer: The contents of this book reflect the views of the editor, the author and the translator. The Tamil Nadu Textbook and Educational Services Corporation is not responsible for the same.

This is a work of fiction. The names, characters and incidents portrayed in it are the work of the author's imagination. Any resemblance to actual persons, living or dead, events or localities, is entirely coincidental.

Printed at: Niyogi Offset Pvt. Ltd., New Delhi, India

Contents

Foreword

Joseph Frank wrote a 2500-page biography of Fyodor Dostoevsky. The world celebrates that biography. We don't have such biographies in Tamil. The great poet Bharathiar does not have such a detailed biography.

Pudumaipithan was a writer who gambled with life and saw its depths. He faced crises, and a lot of pain. He wrote with humour, moral anger, and with a critical outlook. This is the identity of a true artist.

Pudumaipithan's friend T.M.C. Ragunathan wrote this short biography of Pudumaipithan in 1951, as a means of mobilizing funds for Pudumaipithan's family. According to A.R. Venkatachalapathy this book was completed by the author in ten days.

This book talks about the early days of the writer, his arrival in Chennai, his days as a sub-editor in *Dinamani*, his days in the film industry, his experience in Pune on the day of Mahatma Gandhi's assassination, his tryst with tuberculosis, and his friendships. We get to visualize the rare personality that was Pudumaipithan, through these pages.

Pudumaipithan believed that he could make a living by writing, and came to Chennai believing this. He carried deep wounds from his tussles with his father in Tirunelveli. Life in Chennai sent him on a whirlwind tour into a new reality.

Dark is the path
Dark is the mind
In thought and knowledge
Pitch Dark

This is how he visualized his life's journey. Despite such darkness, he sustained his enthusiasm. He converted his life-experiences into stories.

'The life of Pudumaipithan has an air of melancholy, a warning to living writers,' says T.M.C. Ragunathan. That is a fact. Ragunathan knew a hundred times more about Pudumaipithan, than what is written in this book. But circumstances did not allow him to write everything.

So he summarized the life of Pudumaipithan in this book. Ragunathan has an interesting style of writing, which is the beauty of this book.

We want to see a detailed biography of Pudumaipithan. That will be an honour we can offer this great artist.

The Government of Tamil Nadu is publishing the books of nationalized authors. It is a commendable work. It will take the life story of Pudumaipithan to a new generation of readers. I appreciate the work of Tamil Nadu Textbook and Educational Services Corporation in the service of the Tamil language.

—S. Ramakrishnan
Sahitya Akademi Award-winning author,
October 28, 2021.

Foreword to the First Edition

The life of Pudumaipithan has an air of melancholy, of being a warning to living writers.

Pudumaipithan Varalaaru or 'Pudumaipithan's History' should have been published immediately after he passed away. However, I could not gather some crucial information about his life soon enough. It took more than a year to do that. The name of Pudumaipithan reverberated across Tamil Nadu a while ago. I wanted to make the most of the moment and so, I have brought the book out. I wanted to write it more elaborately. But I did not want to delay it. I am satisfied that I could write it in a simple form.

When I started writing this book, I had many embarrassments. Pudumaipithan lived with us, and had passed away recently. His friends and enemies are still living among us. Pudumaipithan's wife and friends do not know about some aspects of his life, which I have mentioned in this book. I avoided mentioning the names of many people. At the same time, I have quoted many people. I skipped instances that could be considered offensive and wrote about relatively palatable events. Some may still think I could have avoided a few stories from the writer's life. I don't want the biography of Pudumaipithan to be an emaciated child. It should have the flourishing aspect of a healthy baby. Pudumaipithan is no more. I have faith that those stories won't be amplified by people.

Many friends, editors, and writers helped me write this book. Just as the squirrel and Hanuman helped Lord Rama, all of them supported me in small and big ways. I thank all of them. I am particularly grateful to Kamalambal, the wife of Pudumaipithan, Thiruvananthapuram S. Chidambaram, and Pudumaipithan's father, Chokkalingam Pillai, for cooperating with me and helping me complete this book.

—Ragunathan
September 1951

The Clan

170 Royapettah High Road, Chennai, was the address of the house where Pudumaipithan lived. One night in the year 1946, while Pudumaipithan and I were chatting, a Tamil poet, whose poetry Pudumaipithan disliked, walked in. After some conversation, the poet lamented, 'What Chovi? The people of Tamil Nadu do not appreciate your stories and my poetry. You and I were born a thousand years ahead.' Chovi was Pudumaipithan's nickname.

Pudumaipithan replied, 'Yes, you were born a thousand years later. I was born a thousand years ahead. How will today's Tamil Nadu understand either of us?'

What a blow for the poet.

Pudumaipithan grudged the fact that Tamil Nadu did not realize that he was a master storyteller. But today, long after his death, Tamil Nadu organizes a festival for him and is celebrating him. Today, Tamil Nadu appreciates the genius of Pudumaipithan. So, he was not born a thousand years ahead of his time. Maybe he was born five years ahead of his time.

Pudumaipithan alias Cho. Vriddhachalam was not born a thousand years ahead. He was not born five years ahead. He was born fifty years ago at the beginning of this century. In twentieth-century Tamil literature, Pudumaipithan was a unique talent, a new light.

Four generations ago, Ulagalantha Perumal of the Shaivaite Vellala community (a vegetarian community in southern Tamil Nadu) from the Tirunelveli region, went to South Arcot. He found work as an accountant in a village where there lived an Englishman, who was serving the court in Vriddhachalam. Pillai had a great affection for the Englishman. Pillai's honesty, relentlessness, and hard work brought him close to the Englishman. The Englishman made Ulagalantha Perumal Pillai a *tehsildar*. The Englishman could not get the name 'Ulagalantha Perumal Pillai' right. It wasn't easy for a white man to pronounce.

The Englishman suggested to Ulagalantha Perumal Pillai that he name himself after the town. As a gesture of gratitude to the man who offered him a great position, Pillai changed his name. He was now Vriddhachalam Pillai. The grandson of the grandson of this Vriddhachalam Pillai was Cho. Vriddhachalam alias Pudumaipithan. Pudumaipithan's ancestor changed his name as per the wish of an Englishman. Cho. Vriddhachalam changed his name to Pudumaipithan to write stories.

Since the time of Ulagalantha Perumal Pillai, the family has been serving the revenue department of the government with unflinching loyalty. Chokkalingam Pillai, Pudumaipithan's father, was born to Vriddhachalam Pillai, the grandson of Ulagalantha Perumal and Alagammai.

Chokkalingam Pillai earned a B.A. degree and then married Parvathathammal. He was a *tehsildar*, in the Land Registration Department, in the district of South Arcot, at the time of his marriage. Chokkalingam Pillai had a transferable job. He had been posted in several places.

It was in 1906, on 25th April, that Pudumaipithan was born in Thiruppathipuliyur near Cuddalore. He was named after his grandfather Vriddhachalam Pillai, following the tradition in Tamil Nadu.

Parvathathammal, the mother of Pudumaipithan, gave birth to a girl child after Pudumaipithan. She passed away in 1914. Pudumaipithan was just eight years old then. He never experienced a mother's love and always remembered this misfortune.

Pudumaipithan's younger sister is Rukmani alias Chellathammal. She married another man named Vriddhachalam Pillai. He was a wildlife officer. He worked in the Cuddappah district. After retirement, he lived in Palayamkottai in Tirunelveli with his family.

Tehsildar Chokkalingam Pillai remarried after the demise of Parvathathammal, and had three sons with his second wife. He remains healthy and fit at ninety-three years, reads without glasses, and does not require a stick to walk around. He speaks clearly. I am reminded of Pudumaipithan whenever I see him. His gesture, speech, and smile resemble Pudumaipithan's. Chokkalingam Pillai is not just a *tehsildar.* He is an author. He wrote a multi-volume book called *Indo-European Races.* He is writing the third volume of the book at this age. Every volume is as heavy as a dictionary.

Pudumaipithan's father gets upset if someone asks him, 'Are you the father of Vriddhachalam?' This was Pudumaipithan's original name. He wants them to ask, 'Is your son Vriddhachalam?' Chokkalingam Pillai is a true-blue loyalist of the British Empire, from the 19th century to the present. He is an Anglophile. He dedicated his book to King George V.

> 'Vriddhachalam is a studious boy. Even when he was young, he memorized *Kandhar Kalivenba* [Devotional poetry in praise of Lord Muruga of Tiruchendur]. I wanted him to translate my work into Tamil. But he did not respect me. That is the way it is. It is because of his birth star. Uncontrollable. Children of this age are like this. As they enter adulthood, they want their fathers to die. Like a young plantain tree killing its mother. What else can I say?'

When Pudumaipithan passed away in 1948, I met his father. That was when he said this to me. He goes on and on once he starts talking. If you are even a little impatient, you cannot listen to him. You require phenomenal patience to bear with him.

In School

His father Chokkalingam Pillai worked as a *tehsildar* in the South Arcot district. Pudumaipithan had to go to school there. As his father kept getting transfers at his job, he was shifted from one school to another. His education could not stabilize because of such frequent transfers. He was not just a pampered child. He was a wild child. Around 1915-16, he studied in the primary schools in Ginjee, Tindivanam, and Kallakurichi. Pudumaipithan could not concentrate on his studies. His mind would waver. 'I loved roaming around in the Ginjee fort. I hated school,' is exactly how Pudumaipithan himself described it later in his life.

Chokkalingam Pillai retired from service in 1918 and he moved to his native town of Tirunelveli. He settled down in Vannarpettai, which is on the southern banks of the Tamirabarani River, and continues to live there. Pudumaipithan was twelve when Chokkalingam Pillai arrived in Tirunelveli. That is the age when the innocence of childhood disappears and the formation of knowledge takes place. His father's long stay in one place stabilized Pudumaipithan's education. The Tamil language may have been born in the North of Tamil Nadu, but it was nourished in the South. Similarly, Pudumaipithan may have been born in the town of Thiruppathipuliyur, yet he was nourished in Tirunelveli. It is Mother Tamirabarani who gives birth to scholars, poets, and writers throughout history. The same mother shaped Pudumaipithan into a beloved son of Mother Tamil.

Pudumaipithan's schooling continued at St. John's school in Tirunelveli. His academic performance in the school was not excellent. But he did gain fantastic insights, useful for a life of writing. He hated the textbooks prescribed for education. Yet, he was in love with other books. He disliked the bookish and impractical knowledge he acquired during his school years. After school, he joined the Hindu college in Tirunelveli.

Hindu College is situated just opposite the railway terminus in Tirunelveli. The great poet Mahakavi Subramania Bharathiar studied in this college. Bharathiar is said to have told his teacher that it wouldn't rain just because Teacher Kalamegam ordered so.

Pudumaipithan did not pay attention to his studies in college. He was engrossed in reading novels. He finished reading a thriller almost every day. As he kept reading novels, he also realized he wanted to write novels himself. During his college days, he had written a thriller. He had confided this to me. This is how the story begins. A Persian merchant reaches the Thoothukudi port. He carries a suitcase. He meets with a rich man in Thoothukudi. He talks business with the rich man. He wants to sell fragrances. The rich man smells a sample of attar given by the merchant. He faints on smelling the scent. The merchant loots his money and runs away. It was not scent but anesthesia. He is not a merchant but a thief.

Pudumaipithan could not recall the spy thriller story completely. It is good that Pudumaipithan did not pursue his interest in spy thriller fiction. He did not follow in the footsteps of thriller fiction authors such as Vaduvoor Iyengar and Arani Mudaliar. Instead, he created amazing short stories that made the Tamil language proud.

Pudumaipithan's father did not realize the truth behind his son's mad obsession with novels. He thought that his son was studying seriously. Pudumaipithan would read novels till two o'clock in the morning. His father Chokkalingam Pillai was extremely happy that his son was reading until early morning. Pillai condemns other children for not reading enough. He condemns Pudumaipithan for reading at untimely hours.

Pudumaipithan could not complete his college education on time because of his weak track record in schooling. He was mischievous in college as well. He wrote some comments about one of his teachers on the blackboard. It was about Professor V. Ponnusamy Pillai, the history professor and vice-principal of the college.

This is what Pudumaipithan wrote on the board:

Mussolini is a dictator of Italy,

Our V.P. is the dictator of Notes!

Only the students who learned history from this professor will understand the complete meaning of this piece of humour. V.P. refers to both Vice-Principal and V. Ponnusamy Pillai.

Tender Coconut Water and Literature

Pudumaipithan was interested in creative literature since his college days. He had friends with whom he could talk literature. Apart from literature, he was keen on playing games. Not games like football and hockey. He was not interested in sports. He was an emaciated child from the start. He was not fit to participate in the school games. So he spent time playfully with his literary friends.

K.S. Sonachalam, the present auditor of the Madras Presidency, A. Muthusivan, who passed away recently after working as a Tamil Professor in Karaikudi Alagappa College, Theetharappan (Theepan), who has already passed away and was the son of the writer T.K.C., Karmayogi Sadanandar, Malleswaram from Bangalore, Guhan Pillai, and Maharajan, were Pudumaipithan's friends in younger days.

Muthusivan lived in a room in Vannarpettai and went to college. That room was the regular haunt of

Pudumaipithan. Many people were part of that team. The commander was Pudumaipithan. Everyone on the team had to follow his instructions. This was how it went:

The room has a mat and mattress. Pudumaipithan will not let the inmates use them. 'The body will be burnt after we die. You can sleep on the floor.' He will make them sit and meditate on palmyra mats. He also sleeps on the floor. Then, there will be a literary discussion. There is also a discussion on theft. It is not about literary theft but about the theft of tender coconut.

There is a coconut grove behind the room they stay in. The milk-white moon sheds a silky light. The coconut leaves move gently in the breeze. The moonlight shines through the leaves. It is a beautiful sight for the literary aficionados. Pudumaipithan enjoyed tender coconut more than this romantic sight. You have to feed yourself. If you climb the trees and pluck the coconuts, the noise will wake up the watchman. He taught his colleagues how to deliver the coconuts without any sound. He trained them in the use of ropes in the process. After learning the techniques, they started plucking coconuts at night. They will carry the coconuts to a nearby field. The croaks of frogs and the squeaks of rats from the mouths of snakes do not deter them from having tender coconut water.

He does it every day.

Pudumaipithan had a nickname. He was called Paramahamsar by his friends. The reason was that he used a lot of metaphors while advising friends. This was only for the daytime. In the evening, he took the avatar of Thirumangai Alwar, one of the twelve Vaishnavite saints. It is an avatar suitable for the theft of coconuts. Thirumangai Alwar wanted to help the devotees of Lord Vishnu through hook or crook. He robbed people and supported the devotees.

They wouldn't return to the room after having the tender coconut water. Pudumaipithan convinced his colleagues that it was against dharma to come back to the room after having such a delectable feast. The banks of the Tamirabarani were a great place to have a nice sleep. There was the mango grove on the river bank. Or the cremation ground next to the grove. The friends encouraged this strange behavior in Pudumaipithan.

This is how Pudumaipithan spent his young days. You can see the traces of this life in his short story 'Sayangala Mayakkam' (Dizzy Evening).

Wedding

Pudumaipithan could not complete his college education in the stipulated period. His obsession with reading fiction and philosophy, stealing tender coconuts, and sleeping in the crematorium, took a toll on his studies. After many a struggle, he finished the undergraduate course in 1931 and got a B.A. degree to add after his name.

The family of Chokkalingam Pillai has been in government jobs for generations. 'Even if it is a quarter rupee salary a month, it should come from a government job,' is a belief that runs deep in the family. True to the middle-class ideal of finding a government job, Chokkalingam Pillai had dreams of making his son a *tehsildar* like him. But by the time Pudumaipithan finished his B.A. degree, he was well past 25 years of age. Age had become a stumbling block for the family's aspirations. Chokkalingam Pillai did not give up. He used all his influence and reached even the governor's office in pursuit of his dreams but to no avail. Pudumaipithan was not keen on using his powers of writing and imagination in the service of a government symbolized by red tape.

Chokkalingam Pillai did not stop because he could not get his son a government job. He wanted Pudumaipithan to study law and become an advocate. Pudumaipithan had also reached the age of marriage. His father decided to kill two birds with one stone. He decided he would ask his son's in-laws to bear the cost of his son's law education. Trivandrum has a law college. So he found a suitable girl in that city for his son.

Chokkalingam Pillai held talks with P.T. Subramaniam Pillai, who was a Public Works Department supervisor in Trivandrum, to give the latter's daughter Kamalambal in marriage to Pudumaipithan. He was so happy that the girl's family had agreed to invest in Pudumaipithan's further studies in law. Pudumaipithan said this to me about this marriage:

> 'At that age, I used to go to the riverbank to smoke a cigar. I was hurrying to the riverbank on that day, having felt the urge to smoke. Dad stopped me and told me about the marriage

> plan. I said yes and went to the riverbank. The engagement was settled. Upon seeing her for the first time, I fell in love with her eyes. I felt that she was the best fit for me because of her beautiful eyes. I call her Kamala Kanna (the one who is my beloved eye). In my letters also, I address her as Kannal (the one with beautiful eyes).'

In the Kollam year 1107, on Ani 31 (July 1931 CE) Kamalambal and Pudumaipithan got married.

Dark is the Route

Pudumaipithan's wedding went according to the plan of his father. But the idea of making Pudumaipithan a law graduate did not materialize. Pudumaipithan did not enjoy his college education so much. He was bitter about it. He did not like the idea of going to college again after marriage. He had developed a deep interest in literature during his college days. He wanted to pursue his interest in literature. He hated the thought of engaging with the Indian Penal Code.

He continued to live as he wished after marriage. He went to a shop near Tirunelveli Junction (close to the river bridge) for literary discussions. Muthiah Pillai Bookshop at Tirunelveli Junction was quite famous in those days. The shop owner was very interested in literature. So, Muthiah Pillai Bookshop became a hub of activity for writers and readers. It was known as 'shop club' as people often gathered here for literary conversations. Tamil scholars P. Sri Acharya and

S. Vaiyapuri Pillai also participated in the discussions at this hub. Pudumaipithan was among the several regular literary enthusiasts who frequented this center.

Pudumaipithan loved writing and literary conversations, and considered it a way of life. His father did not like it. The father felt that Pudumaipithan did not fulfill the dreams he had for him and was wasting time in pursuit of a literary career. 'He has finished his education. He is married. Now it is time for him to do some work and earn money. He loiters around town, and comes back home for food. How long can we feed him?' This was the refrain typical of Father Chokkalingam Pillai.

Senior Pillai's attitude hit Pudumaipithan very hard. Pudumaipithan had been under the care of his stepmother ever since he had lost his mother. We may have read about the tyranny of stepmothers in stories, and seen them in films. We always wonder if such depictions are accurate or exaggerated. In reality, there might be a loving stepmother. Pudumaipithan's stepmother was one in the crowd of tyrannical stepmothers. He endured torture at her hands for a long time. His father's decision to rebuke Pudumaipithan opened new pathways for the stepmother to step up her antics. Pudumaipithan had never seen love in his stepmother. The fact that her anger and aversion became blatant after his marriage hurt Pudumaipithan badly.

It was just one year since the marriage. Conflicts between the mother and daughter-in-law became common. The stepmother rebuked Pudumaipithan both indirectly and openly. She used expressions like 'the adventure of the new wife,' 'secret encouragement offered by wife', and 'wife has become the big woman of the family' to taunt him. Senior Pillai used the worst names – 'useless fellow,' 'misfit,' 'lazybones,' 'liability,' and 'irresponsible fellow' – to address him.

Pudumaipithan was a free-spirited person. So he decided to pursue his literary career without budging an inch because of the pressure tactics of Senior Pillai. He desired to go and join a magazine somewhere. He thought about it single-mindedly and searched for such opportunities, he kept writing stories. He wrote letters to publications. He persisted in reading, writing, and loitering. His stepmom and dad considered him crazy because his activities were not remunerative. Before C. Vriddhachalam became Pudumaipithan, which means 'the one crazy about the modern,' it was his folks at home who considered him a crazy young man.

Pudumaipithan thought that his home was turning into hell for him. Stepmom's tyranny, his father's anger, and the resultant disrespect, led others at home to use abusive language against him. It hurt him deeply. He did not find peace. His mind could not rest calmly.

Water, when heated to a certain temperature, boils over. Do we know the exact moment of its boiling? Pudumaipithan's state of mind was nearing the boiling point. He was hurt repeatedly by the harsh language used by the members of the family. He did not know when his mind would boil over.

Then came that night.

Dad and stepmom were hurling abuses at him as usual. Pudumaipithan listened to all of them. The volcano inside him – which had burned over several years – boiled over. 'I will not stay in this house anymore,' said Pudumaipithan. 'It is alright if you get lost somewhere,' said the old man. But how could he go without anything in hand? Pudumaipithan's in-laws had given cash instead of jewels during the wedding. He asked his father to give him that cash. Senior Pillai refused to give him the money. The altercation escalated. Chokkalingam Pillai did not blink. Pudumaipithan decided to leave.

That was it. Pudumaipithan left home with Kamalambal in the middle of the night. He thought of his future only after reaching the street. He does not have money; he does not have a job; he ceases to have the support of the family from now on; he has the responsibility of taking care of his wife. Where does he go from here? What will he do? He does not have answers.

'Dark is the route. Dark is the mind. Dark is the thought.' These are the lines written by Pudumaipithan. He stood in this same darkness at this moment. He held Kamalambal's hand tight and walked past Vannarapettai toward Murugan Kurichi. They walked two miles and reached his uncle Subramania Pillai's home in Palayamkottai. He stayed there that night, and for a few more days.

Chokkalingam heard the news that his son had stayed at his brother's house. He fought with Subramaniam Pillai and asked him to chase away Pudumaipithan. The writer's uncle did not heed that request. But the uncle could not keep Pudumaipithan and Kamalambal forever. Pudumaipithan also considered it a temporary arrangement. They had to leave now.

So, Pudumaipithan and Kamalambal went to

Thiruvananthapuram, the hometown of Kamalambal. Feeling disgraced, Pudumaipithan wanted to take revenge on his family. The urge to take revenge dominated his thoughts. He could not stay too long in his wife's home. How could a family support a jobless son-in-law for long? Kamalambal and Pudumaipithan left Thriuvananthapuram without a plan. They took the train and reached Madurai. They spent a few days there. Then they spent a few days in Dindigul. They found some relatives to accommodate them in these places. Rejected by folks at home and by in-laws, they found themselves disrespected by relatives. It felt like hell for Pudumaipithan every moment. He sent his wife to her home in Thiruvananthapuram. He told her that he would take her to his place once he found a job. He continued his journey in search of a writing job.

Starting in Chennai

Pudumaipithan had suffered immensely since he left home. The suffering did not deter him from his passionate pursuit of a literary career. He went after it earnestly.

It was after 1930, a time in Indian history when both the political and literary landscapes shifted phenomenally. Mahatma Gandhi transformed the nationalist movement into a popular movement. Congress gained popular support and strengthened itself across the country due to this transformation. The press identified themselves with the goals of Mahatma Gandhi and participated in the political movement, desiring to win freedom for the country. Mahakavi Subramania Bharathiar had left the world already, singing 'When will our thirst for freedom be fulfilled?' Bharathiar's songs saw a revival again at this time. Understanding the emerging nationalist sentiment among the public, some new journals hit the market. Prominent among them were *Gandhi*, edited by T.S. Chockalingam, *Manikodi*, edited by K. Srinivasan, and *Suthanthira Sanku*, edited by Sanku Subramanian.

Manikodi was the last to make an appearance in this lot. It was in September 1933 that *Manikodi* was born. *Gandhi* and *Suthanthira Sanku* were seniors in the business. *Gandhi* used popular and aggressive language to fan anti-imperialist sentiments. It did not give space for literature in the beginning. Awareness of literature was very limited at that time. Politics dominated daily conversations. *Manikodi* was born with the twin aim of promoting both politics and literature. *Manikodi* journalists equated the arrival of their magazine to the birth of a star to dispel darkness.

Stalin Srinivasan alias Manikodi Srinivasan was the editor of the magazine. Varadarajan Ramasamy (Va. Ra) assisted him by writing serious prose, as well as popular columns. Having substance was not considered a virtue at the time. These magazines, however, had genuine energy and drive. A new breed called 'Manikodi Writers' emerged during this time. P.S. Ramiah, Na. Pichamurthy, and Pe. Ko. Sundararajan (City) wrote regularly for *Manikodi*. T. Janakiraman and Sanku Subramanian wrote regularly for *Suthanthira Sanku*. They are distinguished from the *Manikodi* writers.

The situation of magazines in those days was worse than today. The investment was very little; the excitement was too much. We never lacked excitement. If all the printed magazines were sold, we thought it was a huge success. But even if all the copies were sold, when the maths was done, the profit would be zilch. Pudumaipithan thought of making this his career at such a precarious time. He sent his creative works to *Manikodi* and *Gandhi*. He did not expect any payment for writing. He was new to writing. Getting his works published was his priority. 'A new born carrying his umbilical cord on his shoulder and walking in the street, shouting slogans, is an extraordinary scenario.' This is his description of Isakki Muthu in a story titled 'Avatar.' This description fits Pudumaipithan's entry into the literary scene. He needed money for a living. The magazines did not have money to pay him.

Gandhi magazine started a debate on love at first sight. It tried to figure out if 'love at first sight' is real or fake. This debate helped Pudumaipithan enter the world of literature. He mocked love at first sight in an essay called 'Gulab Jamun Love.' *Gandhi* published it. T.S. Chockalingam, the editor of *Gandhi*, and Pudumaipithan started connecting after this. Varadarajan Ramasamy (Va. Ra) read the essay and appreciated it in a letter to Pudumaipithan. Thereafter, they continued the correspondence.

Pudumaipithan wrote stories for *Gandhi* and *Manikodi*. The story 'Ponnagaram' discussed the idea of chastity through a character called Ammalu. 'Kavanthan and Kaman,' another short story, studied the identity of a sex worker. The short story 'Aan Singam' introduced a weak character, Seema. *Manikodi* carried these stories. Pudumaipithan became the subject of discussion when the stories got published. Some people were shocked by the fiery creative spirit of the new writer. Some people appreciated the newness, the pace, and the new perspective of his stories.

Pudumaipithan appeared as a burst of new sunshine on the literary sky. Not like moonlight, which lets you glimpse the other stars. His sun-like brightness dimmed other stars. Pudumaipithan's name resonated with a vast number of readers. Literary editors wanted to understand and interact with him.

Pudumaipithan created such amazing literature at a time when he had left home and was struggling for a livelihood. Surviving from day to day was a challenge for him. *Manikodi* and *Gandhi* could publish his works but could not employ him. Pudumaipithan was keen on coming to Chennai. He kept writing to Va. Ra about it. Va. Ra explained why it would not be a sustainable idea. Pudumaipithan's desire to be in Chennai was as strong as the Shaivite saint Nandanar's devotion to the deity Thillai Nataraja, the Lord of Chidambaram. Immensely strong and hence unstoppable.

Va. Ra and Chockalingam did not stand to lose anything if Pudumaipithan arrived. But the challenge was in sustaining another livelihood in the city. *Manikodi* was popular but its economic foundations were shaky. The magazine struggled to survive because there was no capital to support it. Those who were associated with the magazine also stared at an uncertain future. The literary workers who already faced serious difficulties in Chennai did not want to pass on the same woe to Pudumaipithan.

Pudumaipithan landed in Chennai one fine morning without giving any prior notification to his friends. He met Chockalingam and Va. Ra as soon as he landed. He became one with them from that day onwards. They could not abandon him. They could not help him either.

It was an embarrassing situation for the *Manikodi* team. However, neither the ambitious Pudumaipithan nor the *Manikodi* management worried about it. The socialist idea of sharing whatever they could get propelled them forward. Most of the time, they did not have anything to share except hunger.

The following is what Va. Ra told me about the arrival of Pudumaipithan in Chennai:

> 'He landed suddenly one day. We did not have much money. We could not say no to him. We gave him two rupees. That was for his food expenses. He did the most unexpected thing with it. He went to Moore Market and bought a book by Guy De Maupassant for one rupee seventy-five paisa, and spent the rest of the money on a Spencer cigar. When I asked him what he would do for food, he did not give it much thought. He lit the cigar and started reading the book.'

This is how the Chennai life of Pudumaipithan began.

Work at *Oozhiyan*

Manikodi was an experiment with truth for Pudumaipithan, and for the others involved in the venture. He did not continue there. He worked in *Manikodi* without any pay. Then he got an opportunity to work with a salary elsewhere. Raya Chockalingam published a magazine called *Oozhiyan* from Karaikudi. Pudumaipithan became a sub-editor at *Oozhiyan*. In the middle of 1934, the magazine shifted its headquarters to Chennai.

Oozhiyan focused on social reforms and published Raya Chockalingam's old-style lyrics along with some essays and stories. *Oozhiyan*'s editorial policies were not in complete alignment with Pudumaipithan's. However, Pudumaipithan needed financial support to sustain his life in Chennai. His short stories 'Ahalya,' 'Thekkankandrugal,' and 'Theruvilakku' were published in *Oozhiyan*.

Pudumaipithan could not hold on to the sub-editor post in *Oozhiyan* for long. His independent thinking continued to pose challenges to his career. Esakkimuthu Sivam (E. Sivam) from Nagercoil was his colleague in *Oozhiyan*. E. Sivam was his senior and wrote short stories. Sivam felt embarrassed that his junior was writing better short stories than him. It soured the relationship between them. Sivam wanted to dominate Pudumaipithan. Pudumaipithan wanted to leave the magazine and was waiting for an opportunity to do that. He hesitated because it was the first paid gig for him in Chennai. He would be out on the streets again if he left the position. But then, he was least bothered about the consequences of his actions. He ended his relationship with the magazine and left the job soon enough.

Pudumaipithan did not discuss the question of his leaving the job with his friends. He only explained the particular circumstance that led to the parting. 'I asked for a dictionary to do translation work. I said it would be nice to have a dictionary in the office. They told me that since I had a B.A. degree, I didn't need a dictionary. I realized the precarious position I was in and left the job.' This was how he described the moment of his leaving.

He had to find refuge somewhere to sustain his literary career. He came back to Chennai to realize this goal.

When Pudumaipithan met Va. Ra (Varadarajan Ramasamy) in Chennai, the latter asked, 'How is E. Sivam?'

'E' means fly in Tamil. 'Fly Sivam has become Ant Sivam and has bitten me hard,' said Pudmaipithan angrily, with a tinge of sarcasm.

Both Va. Ra and Pudumaipithan laughed about this spontaneous reaction.

Pudumaipithan stayed in Chennai to pursue his career in writing.

Manikodi's Fall

'*Kettum Pattanam Ser*' is a Tamil proverb. It means that migrating to a city, even at a cost or loss, is good. But Chennai city has never been a fountainhead of food and wealth, to validate this saying. Those who wish to make money can make it anywhere. The noble goals of life and the hunger for food force us in opposite directions. It is no surprise that the *Gandhi* magazine, founded with some of the highest ideals, could not go on because of financial distress. *Gandhi* merged with *Manikodi* at the end of 1934. This merger only strengthened the bond between Varadarajan Ramasamy, T.S. Chockalingam, and K. Srinivasan, but it did not help *Manikodi*. Every day was a trial by fire for the magazine.

Pudumaipithan came back to Chennai at this point. *Manikodi*'s finances were already bad. It was getting worse by the day. Pudumaipithan and P.S. Ramiah tried their hand at keeping it going, along with the trio mentioned in the last paragraph. Everyone at *Manikodi* led an austere life, and could never expect a monthly pay. That did not alter their determination. They wanted to promote literature in novel ways. They announced competitions and prizes in the service of literature. They did not promote rationalism. At that time, Kalki Krishnamurthy (the author of the classic *Ponniyin Selvan*, a fictional account of historic figure Rajaraja Chola) was the editor of *Ananda Vikatan* magazine. *Manikodi* authors and Kalki had a great exchange of letters on the question of rationalism. *Manikodi* conducted essay and short story competitions. The patrons of *Manikodi* sponsored the prizes.

A short story competition had the title: 'How to keep up energy levels in crises?' The prize money was ten rupees. Adhikudi K. Ramachandran, an author, wrote a story titled 'Test' and won the competition. He went on to be part of the story department at Gemini Studios. The *Manikodi* writers might not have known about the other competitions and other prize winners. Ramachandran worked briefly for *Manikodi* as well.

Whatever the tricks employed by the promoters of *Manikodi*, the issue of sustenance haunted them. The magazine could not go on. K. Srinivasan, the founding editor of *Manikodi*, joined *Bombay Standard* as its editor. T.S. Chockalingam became the editor of *Dinamani*, a Tamil daily belonging to the *Indian Express* group. Varadarajan Ramasamy (Va. Ra) worked with *Suthanthira Sanku* for some time. He then went to Colombo and became the sub-editor of *Virakesari*.

Although the founder left *Manikodi*, Pudumaipithan and P.S. Ramiah sustained it for a little more time. The future remained a mystery for Pudumaipithan and Ramiah in the event of the closure of *Manikodi*. They wanted to sustain the magazine for their identity. At the same time, they worried not just about discontinuing a literary tradition but also about the loss of their livelihoods. *Manikodi* may not have brought them great prosperity. But it was an occupation they loved. It was something they were passionate about. Even after Srinivasan left, the writers continued running *Manikodi*.

Pudumaipithan narrated the story of running the magazine to me one day:

> '*Manikodi* came under our control. The dues to the printing press were 18.75 Rupees. The dues to be collected were not as much. They didn't come in regularly. Hunger was not an issue. We were used to it. Athikudi K. Ramachandran

> came and joined us. The printing press guy kept pressurizing us for money. The table and chairs in the office were all rented. The owners didn't get the rent. We told the printing person that if only he printed the magazine, would he recover the money from us. The printer obliged. Rarely, a subscriber or an honest agent, would send a money order for three or four rupees. We were nobles on the day the money order arrived. We would go to Ramakrishna Lunch Home to eat. We would come back and continue our literary service. On the days without money orders, we expected one of our friends to help. Chidambaram Subramanian who wrote regularly for *Manikodi,* worked many jobs and got a monthly pay. When he visited the office, we would get coffee and food. Once, both Ramiah and I thought of selling peppermint and beedi instead of suffering like this.'

Under Pudumaipithan and P.S. Ramiah, *Manikodi* reduced its size and pages. The magazine shunned political content and became full of short stories. Pichamoorthi, Ku. Pa. Rajagopalan, Citi, C.S.

Chellappa, and Elangovan wrote regularly in *Manikodi.* Chidambara Subramanian, Ka. Na. Subramanian, P.M. Kannan, and Mouni joined the *Manikodi* family.

The struggle for sustenance, motivation, and the thrill of doing literary service kept them going for some time. In the absence of a sustenance plan, the magazine cannot be continued. *Manikodi* shuttered in April 1936. It became imperative to find livelihoods for the people associated with the magazine. Chettiar, the owner of the *Virakesari* newspaper from Colombo, visited Chennai at that time. Va. Ra was already a sub-editor there. The owner of *Virakesari* wanted to take some of Va. Ra's colleagues to Colombo for work. Pudumaipithan once recounted to me the moment of Chettiyar's arrival in Chennai. 'Chettiyar does not come for recruitment. He comes for cheap labor. It is as cunning as a manager coming to find indentured labour for tea estates.'

Pudumaipithan did not want to go to *Virakesari.* But the arrival of *Virakesari* Chettiyar may have appeared to him as providence at a time when he was struggling for livelihood. The hard situation made him decide in favour of a job in Colombo. He wanted to tell T.S. Chockalingam before leaving for Colombo. A new turning point awaited him there.

'I am joining *Virakesari* in Colombo,' said Pudumaipithan.

'Have you decided on going to Colombo?' asked Chockalingam.

'No other options,' said Pudumaipithan.

'For livelihood? Would you like to join *Dinamani*?' asked Chockalingam.

Pudumaipithan thought about it for a minute. 'Should I go to Colombo? The place is new. The people are new.' He joined *Dinamani* as a sub-editor under T.S. Chockalingam, the editor of the newspaper. It was 1936. Pudumaipithan worked with the newspaper till the end of 1943. T.S. Chockalingam left the organization at the end of 1943. Pudumaipithan was among those who left *Dinamani* with Chockalingam.

Resurrection and Second Death

Manikodi stopped publication in the middle of 1936. But P.S. Ramiah and K. Ramachandran made a determined effort to revive it. Thanks to their efforts, the magazine resumed publication in September 1936.

They wanted to lay strong financial foundations for *Manikodi* to ensure an uninterrupted run of publications. They created a company to publish *Manikodi*, along with literary and political books. P.S. Ramiah and his colleagues worked on this plan for one year. 'Navayuga Prasuralayam' was born as a limited company. It started with an investment of 20,000 Rupees. It was in the beginning of 1937.

The people behind Navayuga Prasuralayam had experience in the business of publishing. The directors included Manikodi Srinivasan from the *Bombay Standard*, and K. Santhanam from *The Indian Express*. The others were S.V. Samy from *The Indian Express*,

A.N. Sivaraman from *Dinamani*, Batlagundu P.S. Sankaran, and P.S. Ramiah. T.S. Chockalingam of *Dinamani* was the managing director. P.S. Ramiah was the managing editor of Navayuga Prasuralayam.

Manikodi restarted her journey under the new banner. The writers who contributed to her pages earlier started writing again. Pudumaipithan also wrote. He wrote *Baktha Kusela*, a play, and 'Nasakara Kumbal,' a short story, for *Manikodi.* Navayuga Prasuralayam published books. Its first book was 'Mahana Suyatchi' (State Autonomy) authored by A.N. Sivaraman. It continued publishing books and made money.

When Navayuga Prasuralyam was doing well, Pa. Ramaswamy (Pa. Ra), an author from Tirunelveli, joined the company. He later became the Municipal Chairperson of Tirunelveli. Chockalingam appointed him as the publisher. P.S. Ramiah, the editor of *Manikodi*, and Pa. Ra could not get along very well. Ramiah grew bitter towards Pa. Ra and Chockalingam. This led to the removal of Ramiah from editorship. Chockalingam, as the managing director, made this decision.

The regular contributions of *Manikodi* writers stopped as Pa. Ra still helmed the magazine. Pa. Ra could only run it for a few years. *Manikodi* ceased publication forever. P.S. Ramiah who had revived the child that was *Manikodi*, buried it forever after a short stint.

In an introduction to his short story collection *Aanmai* in 1947, Pudumaipithan wrote about *Manikodi*:

> 'There were several magazines before the coming of *Manikodi*. There was no magazine before and after *Manikodi* that appreciated innovative literary efforts. K. Srinivasan who founded the *Manikodi* magazine runs a newspaper in another language. In a different state. Is it a punishment transfer? It is a world full of opportunist owls and dubious old tigers. Tamil people don't give a damn about the destruction of their language. I am helpless. The word 'Marumalarchi' (Renaissance) acquired new meaning and pace. Some folks welcomed it. Many made fun of it. Majority of the population do not know about it. The infanticide of *Manikodi* happened due to a financial crunch. It got buried in the municipal garbage bin called indifference. P.S. Ramiah, some friends, and I, resuscitated it. Zeal was our only investment.

> When she attained great beauty after three years, we got a little support from a friend. He sold her to a company. She met with her nirvana there. This is the story of *Manikodi*. This is the story of the people who desired to do new experiments in the Tamil language.'

Besides running *Manikodi*, Navayuga Prasuralayam brought out books in modern Tamil literature. Among the many books it has brought out is *Pudumaipithan Kathaigal* (Pudumaipithan's Stories). The book continues to inspire young people. It is a turning point in Tamil literature. It is the first-ever Tamil book of short stories to carry the name of the author in its title. Navayuga Prasuralayam brought out *Ulagathu Sirugathaikal*, *Nasakara Kumbal*, *Baktha Kusela*. It also published *Aaru Kathaigal*, *Fascist Jadamuni*, and *Cupsip Durbar*. All authored by Pudumaipithan. This series of publications brought fame to the publishing house and the author.

Dinamani and *Dinasari*

Pudumaipithan joined *Dinamani* as a sub-editor following the advice of T.S. Chockalingam. He joined for a meagre salary. The salary he received while leaving *Dinamani* was also inadequate. It was true that Pudumaipithan had attained a respectable position in *Dinamani*. But it had not helped him in improving his quality of life. In *Manikodi*, Pudumaipithan did not know where his next meal was going to come from. In *Dinamani*, he struggled to meet life expenses for the whole month with a paltry sum. The daily demand for translations in *Dinamani* kept him occupied. His literary output dipped because of this preoccupation. He had to keep translating copies from the Associated Press and Reuters. Pudumaipithan enjoyed doing *Dinamani*'s annual publications. They carried his literary works. 'Ninaivu Pathai' is a story from that era.

Readers could see the truth bombs of Pudumaipithan in the book review section in *Dinamani*. Some authors feared this section. He used the pseudonym Rasamattam to pose arguments against the editor of the *Kalki* magazine. Rasamattam's powerful critique of *Kalki* engaged readers.

It was 1943. Chockalingam, the editor, and the management of *Dinamani,* had huge differences of opinion on several issues. This led to the resignation of Chockalingam and his loyalists from the company. Pudumaipithan who had a high regard for Chockalingam, also left. His loyalty took him to where his editor went.

In the beginning of 1944, Chockalingam launched the newspaper *Dinasari.* Pudumaipithan joined the company. For the first time, he got a decent salary in the business of writing. *Dinasari* was a cooperative of sub-editors, the ones who had walked out of *Dinamani* over issues regarding rights. The newspaper provided reasonable pay to the media workers. Pudumaipithan had job satisfaction when he worked for *Manikodi.* But he did not find job satisfaction in *Dinasari,* though he had a decent salary to meet his expenses.

He quit *Dinasari* and waited a few months before taking the plunge into the film industry. His friends wondered why he left the newspaper industry, after having made a name for himself in print media, for over a decade. When anyone asked him about it, he said, 'I exhausted myself in journalism for ten years. I am left with nothing at the end of it. I have a wife and a child. If I join the world of cinema, I will be able to save some money.'

It is true. Many of Pudumaipithan's colleagues entered the film industry and made money. Ilangovan became a leading dialogue writer. P.S. Ramiah earned repute as a filmmaker. 'I have talent. I need not wait for opportunities. I can create opportunities' may have been the thought Pudumaipithan had. His wife Kamalambal felt that her husband had toiled enough without making money. She wished him well in the new venture. What Pudumaipithan said may have been true. But it is not the complete picture.

Pudumaipithan had great respect for Chockalingam Pillai since the days of *Dinamani*. The respect was mutual. Chockalingam understood Pudumaipithan's genius and gave him enormous freedom in writing. Both connected well. The families of both got on well with each other. Kamalambal called Chockalingam 'Appa' (Father). It was an intimate bond. When the going got tough for Chockalingam in *Dinamani*, Pudumaipithan stood by him, defending his editor. He left the institution along with the editor because of the deep relationship they had.

Familiarity breeds contempt. In Tamil, a proverb says that milk tastes sour if you keep drinking it. It may be that the regular habit of drinking milk that leads to such a taste. Or the tongue may have soured. After Pudumaipithan joined *Dinasari*, the relationship between him and Chockalingam turned bitter. We can assume that familiarity was not the reason for this turn of events. It is futile to attempt to discover the origin of discord.

The relationship between Pudumaipithan and *Dinasari*'s sub-editor Venkatarajulu Naidu was normal. Chockalingam showered them with the same love and affection from the beginning. But the camaraderie between Chockalingam and Pudumaipithan hit a wall. It is common for a third party to come and interfere in a relationship between two people. A fourth party interfered in Pudumaipithan's relationship with the editor.

The fourth person was a writer of historic fiction. Some people break the relationship between two people with an expected outcome in mind. Others do it for sadistic pleasure. It is not important to probe the motives of the author of historic fiction. His interference ended the love and affection between Pudumaipithan and Chockalingam. Suspicion is the worst poison. It spreads without making any noise. It pollutes the mind before you even know it. The poison of suspicion spreads fast in both minds. It is beyond repair even sooner.

At this juncture, *Dinasari* carried a critical story on literary publications. The writer has hit out at a publisher known to Chockalingam in this story. Pudumaipithan had cleared the story. Chockalingam called Pudumaipithan and asked him to carry a rejoinder to the story. Chockalingam did not find the rejoinder authored by Pudumaipithan satisfactory. Chockalingam asked Pudumaipithan to come out with a more powerful rejoinder. Pudumaipithan told him the issue did not have enough substance to merit being written on further.

Chockalingam countered Pudumaipithan on this. 'When you wrote in *Dinamani* as Rasamattam, you never got tired of it. Now, you are getting tired on this issue.' Pudumaipithan retorted, 'I got tired of working with you. I am leaving the company.'

This was the journey of Pudumaipithan at *Dinasari*, after his resignation from *Dinamani*. Pudumaipithan never discussed the reasons behind his exit from *Oozhiyan*. He never discussed the precise circumstances in which he exited *Dinasari*. Pudumaipithan's journalism came to an end.

Freedom

In 1933, in Tirunelveli, when his relationship with his father turned bitter, Pudumaipithan had left his home and pursued a career in journalism. For 11 years, he had cut his teeth in the business of news writing, and then left *Dinasari* in 1944. Livelihood was a huge challenge when he first left Tirunelveli. When he left journalism and was nearly 40 years old, livelihood remained a challenge. Yet there was a difference. When he left Tirunelveli, he was just Cho. Viruddhachalam. Now he was Pudumaipithan. A writer who had won the hearts and minds of the Tamil-reading public. Would fame serve as capital to help him earn his livelihood? Now Pudumaipithan found himself in almost the same situation as in the past. When he left Tirunelveli, his situation was turbulent. Now, it was not so shaky. He seized his freedom from *Dinasari*, just as he had severed ties with his father.

In 1943, the Second World War was raging. Chennai (then Madras) feared Japanese bombs so much that the city saw an exodus. People went back to their villages. Pudumaipithan sent his wife back to Tirunelveli. He accompanied her on the trip. He needed a home in Tirunelveli to enable her to stay. He could not afford to have two rented homes – one in Chennai and one in Tirunelveli. His salary as a sub-editor was not that high. Pudumaipithan approached his father Chockalingam Pillai. Chockalingam Pillai was stubborn. He had three or four houses in Tirunelveli. He could have easily given one to his son. He feared that his son would claim ownership if he gave it to him. He refused to give accommodation to Pudumaipithan. The father and the son had parted ways ten years back. When they came together again, there was conflict. Pudumaipithan fought with his father. He wanted either a house or his share of inherited property. In the meantime, Kamalambal lived in a relative's home in Ambasamudram. Kamalambal was not aware of the confrontation between the father and the son. Pudumaipithan wanted to take revenge on his father. So he persisted with the request for a share of the property. Chockalingam Pillai was ready to give only a share of the ancestral property. He was not ready to apportion the properties he had accumulated. Pudumaipithan pointed out that his wife's family had given money as dowry during the wedding. Chockalingam Pillai was firm on his decision. Pudumaipithan too, was determined to take the matter to its logical conclusion. Chockalingam Pillai decided to give his son a share in the ancestral property. He was not willing to give a house or cash. Pudumaipithan asked for cash instead of the remaining share. His father suggested something unique.

'I don't have cash now. Instead, you can take my book *Indo-European Races* and sell them to make money,' said Chockalingam.

Pudumaipithan could write books. He had never been interested in selling books. Moreover, he didn't like his father's book. He refused to sell the stock of books written by his father. 'Your book is not saleable. It is so heavy. No one will buy it,' said Pudumaipithan.

Pudumaipithan had to go to court and get an injunction to recover the cash promised by his father. That is a separate story. After the settlement, Pudumaipithan gave a written assurance to his father that there would be no more claims from his side.

However, Pudumaipithan could not even hold on to the cultivable land he inherited. He sold the land as soon as he left *Dinasari*. He sold it to a Muslim for a low price.

The land was surrounded by the lands of his relatives. 'How can he sell it to someone outside the family? How can he sell it to a Thulukkan (a slur to refer to Muslims)? Sinner. A traitor.' This was the response of the family members to this incident.

Pudumaipithan documented this event as follows:

> 'It is the only opportunity for me to take revenge on the family members. I used it. My family has let me down. I introduced a new owner on the family land so that it would serve as a constant reminder of their sin. Let them remember it every day. Or at least when they face some challenges.'

It was an open declaration of his vendetta.

When Pudumaipithan received cash for the land, his uncle Subramania Pillai advised him to buy a jeep and rent it out. The Second World War was coming to an end. Jeeps were available at reasonable prices. It was useful advice because it would give Pudumaipithan recurring income.

You will be surprised by the answer Pudumaipithan gave to this suggestion. 'I don't have an objection to buying a jeep. I will run over my father with it. Is it okay?' This crude response made Subramania Pillai shut up.

The money helped Pudumaipithan survive a war-hit Chennai. As he was jobless, the money was exhausted gradually. Now, he had to plan for his livelihood again.

Livelihood or Literature?

In his introduction to the short story collection *Kanchanai*, Pudumaipithan says, 'My stories are not an insurance for the future.' His stories may serve the larger common good of humanity. His stories, his literary service, and his journalism did not pay for his creature comforts. His translation and sub-editing work in *Dinamani* and *Dinasari* made him tired. After 11 years of journalistic work, he had to think of new livelihood options. He was thinking of enhancing his economic opportunities. It was no surprise that he had to find new economic avenues to sustain himself.

Literary creation was the only profession he was aware of. The only vehicle for that is a magazine. To believe that a good writer can sustain her livelihood by being a freelance writer is an impossible proposal. 'If you are a writer, you are starving completely. If you are a journalist, you are starving partially,' is a popular saying and a fact. Pudumaipithan had realized this. After many years of writing, he had a few options.

'Livelihood or Literature?' was the question that bothered him the most. He desired both. He wanted life to prosper. He also wanted literature to prosper. He needed hope for the prosperity of life and literature. This thought dominated his mind. For literature to prosper, life has to prosper first. What profession should I choose for that? That is the question.

You need money for a decent living. Even the paltry salary he was getting in the newspapers had stopped. He had to think of making money for each day. He worried about it. The absence of a source of income disturbed him. He could not find answers. He finally determined to try his hand at films.

Why don't I write scripts for films? It is an opportunity to make use of literature. It is also remunerative. I cannot keep starving in the name of a noble cause. I have to sell literature. I cannot paint if there is no wall for me to paint on. I need money for my survival. Once money comes, I can serve the purpose of literature. The source of money is not a problem. I need money now. The money acquired through the sale of a dog will never bark at me. When people who pretend to despise myth-making go behind the scenes, and make money by writing for films, why shouldn't I do it?

He thought like this before entering the world of films. He wanted to make film writing as his profession. Writing for films is not against the noble cause of literature. But the state of Tamil films made him think many times about it. Many film producers wanted to increase their wealth rather than pass on a great message to the masses. Whatever his misgivings, he had to follow the trend if he wanted to survive in the market. His commitment to idealism did not matter in the larger scheme of the industry. So he decided to write for films.

He looked at films as a means to deal with the challenge of livelihood. His commitment to literature remained intact. He quit journalism, but he never quit literature. He wanted to start a magazine for literature after making some money in films. He told me once: 'Dear! Let some money come to us. We will start a literary magazine. Do you know the name of the magazine? It is Sodhanai (Trial).'

The idea of starting the literary magazine occupied his mind. In 1946, his circumstances improved considerably. There was more hope and it seemed to be a favorable situation to start the magazine. I visited Tirunelveli at that time. I received a letter from Pudumaipithan, saying: 'All our desires and plans take shape. I have complete faith they will succeed. Please do not be pessimistic. I am getting more and more work here. I am afraid my attention on the magazine will be reduced.'

If anyone thinks that Pudumaipithan entered films to make money, it is a mistake. He never thought of becoming rich. Later, when he faced a financial crunch, he said this to a friend: 'I don't need money to waste on vanities. I need it for having three meals a day.' It shows how he struggled even for his basic needs.

His financial condition became worse. He could not start the literary magazine he dreamt of. He faced huge challenges.

In the World of Films

Pudumaipithan made up his mind to enter the world of films. He had to contact the right person at the right moment to make it work. This challenge did not last long. The market knows that Pudumaipithan is a good writer. The fact that he left *Dinasari* newspaper is well known. It is no secret that he would like to enter films. He does not have any difficulty in foraying into the film market. Lady Luck came in search of him before he could take the first step.

A new film company had started in Mambalam then. It was called the Balagopal Cinema Company. Balagopal Naidu was the promoter of the company. He came and joined hands with Pudumaipithan. Pudumpaithan was in a financial crisis at the time. Balagopal Naidu gave him an advance of five hundred rupees to write a film story. Even a drizzle is a great gift for the scorched earth. Pudumaipithan was happy that good times had started. But Balagopal Naidu was left in the lurch. The reason was Pudumaipithan.

Filmmaker Murugadasa (A. Muthuswamy) was working in Gemini Studios. He had great regard for the modern literary icons. He is the one who took Ki. Ramachandran and P.S. Ramiah into the story department of the Gemini Studios. Murugadasa was a great fan of Pudumaipithan's works. He shared the struggles and sufferings of *Manikodi's* experiment with Ki.Ramachandran and Pudumaipithan. It is no surprise that Pudumaipithan got a call from the Gemini Studios. Gemini Studios planned to film the life story of Avvai, a popular woman poet of the Sangam Age. The film production house wanted Pudumaipithan to do the film script. Ki. Ramachandran and Pudumaipithan would be collaborators in the writing of the script. Pudumaipithan signed the contract with Gemini Studios. It was not just the lure of money. Two things fascinated Pudumaipithan. First, the opportunity to write the story of Avvai. The work gave him immense satisfaction. Second, Gemini Studios is a reliable institution where your growth is certain. Pudumaipithan needed it. He was happy about writing *Avvai.* He had to leave Balagopal Naidu in the lurch because of this exciting assignment.

I was with Pudumaipithan when he wrote the script for *Avvai.* He showed every bit of his writing before sending it to the company. I still remember many lines written by him for *Avvai*. The writing for the opening scene of the film gives me goosebumps. The scene is one in which Avvai chases away a ghost with a poem that ends with the lines: 'Go Away! Away from here! Far Away from here!' It opens in darkness. Her introduction happens in the darkness. King Chola comes to check on the city in the darkness. They meet in the darkness. The King has seen her chase away a ghost. Though he could not see her face, he understood her mind. 'Mother! Why are you staying in the dilapidated building? Come and stay in the Palace,' said the King. 'Did you say that it is a hollow building? The universe has originated from nothing – a hollow.' It is how Avvai comes to life on the big screen in the words of Pudumaipithan. King Athiyaman gifts Avvai an amla fruit that will give her immortality. 'O King! There is only one way to come into this world. But there are many ways to leave this world. Do you think that this amla fruit can stop all the pathways to death?' This is Avvai's response, in the words of Pudumaipithan.

I have given only a few examples. Pudumaipithan's script was full of such profound conversations. Gemini Studios did not use Pudumaipithan's script. If it could be published as a book, it would be a literary asset to the Tamil-speaking people.

Even as he was writing the script for *Avvai*, Pudumaipithan got an opportunity to write another film script thanks to Murugadasa. Nandalal, the promoter of Baskar Pictures, signed Pudumaipithan up to write a script for the film *Kamavalli*. The money Pudumaipithan received for *Kamavalli* was much higher than the money he got from the Gemini Studios.

The scriptwriting work for *Kamavalli* was underway. The filmmaker, Pudumaipithan, and I went to meet the heroine of the film. Her mother tongue is Telugu. There are Telugu-speaking heroines in Tamil films. Some of them speak better Tamil than Tamil-speaking heroines. This heroine speaks chaste Telugu. She speaks colloquial Tamil. Pudumaipithan had to narrate the story to her. As soon as he came back to the car, he told the filmmaker: 'If she is the only choice for a heroine, can I make her mute? Let not Tamil die on her tongue.' The power of changing the heroine or making her mute is not within the reach of the filmmaker or the scriptwriter. We all laughed at Pudumaipithan's joke.

The opportunity to write scripts for *Avvai* and *Kamavalli* happened in the first part of 1946.

Pudumaipithan believed that he would get many such opportunities in the coming years. He was quite confident of his future in films. He felt overwhelmed by the huge amount of money he received as remuneration. He gifted his wife silk sarees. He bought an expensive gold medal for Dinakari, his daughter, who was born that year.

But the next year, 1947, was unlike the year before. The world of films is a unique universe. We can study the trends of the share market and adjust to its fluctuations. But there are no standards for the whims and fancies of the film producers. Their mood swings knew no bounds. It is no surprise that the year 1947 was not similar to 1946 for Pudumaipithan.

It is not that nothing happened after *Avvai* and *Kamavalli*. Kuppuraj came from Coimbatore. I don't remember if the name of that film was Lakshmi Vijayam or Saraswati Vijayam. He asked Pudumaipithan to write a script based on who is the best – Lakshmi or Saraswati. Pudumaipithan started working on it. He went to Madurai Chitrakala Studio to be part of the filmmaking process. He was in a hotel in Madurai and continued work on the script. One day, he came back to Chennai without any prior notice. I did not expect it. I asked him why. 'An interesting story,' said Pudumaipithan.

'The man did not turn up. I wrote a song and kept it for him just in case he returned. Listen to the song. That is the only interesting part of it,' said Pudumaipithan.

This is the song Pudumaipithan left behind in a hotel room in Madurai.

> 'Going back to Chennai. I will give the story
> Once I am here. Don't dodge by false promises.
> Half the story is here under the pillow. The
> remaining story waits here.'

I realised the developments that must have taken place, from the song.

Pudumaipithan completed the story. He completed most of the dialogue for the film. The film did not happen. So he did not get the money. He published the story with the title 'Vaakkum Vakkum' (Word and Capacity). The people of Tamil Nadu at least got to read the story, though it could not make it to the big screen.

The film Lakshmi Vijayam came and disappeared from Pudumaipithan's life. The grace of Goddess Lakshmi (The Goddess of Wealth) also retracted from his life. Penury visited him again in the first half of 1947. We cannot blame it on Pudumaipithan's extravaganza. Pudumaipithan wanted to make it big using the small earnings he had. It is a sad tale of a gamble that went awry from the beginning.

All of a sudden, a star of wealth appeared in Pudumaipithan's sky. Then it disappeared in a short period. Pudumaipithan lost his savings and struggled every day to make both ends meet. This situation lasted several months.

There was a twist in the tale. Balagopal Naidu came back. He wanted Pudumaipithan to give the promised script. He hurried Pudumaipithan. Whenever Balagopal Naidu came, Pudumaipithan got an opportunity elsewhere. It always ended in heartbreak for Naidu. The first time Naidu came, Pudumaipithan got an opportunity in Gemini Studios. This time he got another opportunity.

He was to write for a film called *Rajamukthi*. It is the last film script written by him.

Rajamukthi is a film produced by M.K. Thyagaraja Bagavathar. Bagavathar's team met Pudumaipithan and requested him to write the script. Pudumaipithan agreed to do it. The team behaved secretively. Even the conversations with Pudumaipithan were hush-hush. The team took Pudumaipithan to Bagavathar's residence in Trichy secretly. Someone else made the booking on the train for him. It may be the trade secret of the film producer. Pudumaipithan signed the contract for *Rajamukthi* in Trichy. He received the advance amount. He returned to Chennai. Pudumaipithan was happy. He and his wife Kamalambal stayed in the Woodlands Hotel, one of the hangouts frequented by the rich and famous of the Chennai city. He started writing the script for *Rajamukthi* there.

Balagopal Naidu visited Pudumaipithan again. It was two years since he gave Pudumaipithan an advance for a story. Pudumaipithan got irritated by the sudden arrival of Naidu. He had to leave for Pune along with the team of Bagavathar the next morning. It is difficult to finish a film script overnight. Pudumaipithan was not in the mood to do that script. But he had promised Naidu that the script would be ready the next day. He burned the midnight oil to do that script. As the Tamil proverb goes, you cannot give birth to a child when you see dried ginger. Dried ginger helps a woman to maintain her heath during pregnancy, and give birth to a healthy child. This does not mean that she can give birth to a child whenever she sees dried ginger. Even if you give birth, the child will be as weak as a piece of dried ginger. The script for Naidu turned out to be very weak. He handed over the script to his wife Kamalambal, and took the train to Pune in the morning.

Naidu arrived in the morning. He read the script written by Pudumaipithan. 'What is this? It looks as if he has written merely to offset the advance amount. How can I do a film with a five-page script?' Naidu could not get Pudumaipithan's attention. That interaction, which Naidu had with Kamalambal, was the last conversation about Naidu's film. When Pudumaipithan boarded the train to Pune, Yama, the Lord of Death, followed him.

Parvathakumari

Pudumaipithan considered Parvatham as a sacred name. That was the name of his mother. When he had to endure the negligence of his father and the autocracy of his stepmother, he always thought of his mother. His mother left him in his childhood. He had given the name of his mother to his only child Dinakari. Yes. The other name of Dinakari is Parvathakumari. This chapter is not about Dinakari. It is about Parvathakumari Productions.

Parvathakumari Productions is the name of the film production company Pudumaipithan founded. He started the company in the same year Dinakari was born. That was 1946. How could Pudumaipithan start a company within a year of joining films? Did he have so much money? Did Pudumaipithan own a film company? His friends are aghast with such questions.

But the experiment called Parvathakumari Productions wreaked havoc on the life of Pudumaipithan.

It sucked his blood. It put his life at risk. He associated sanctimony with the name Parvatham. Contrary to the value he associated with the name, it became a nightmare; a liability.

I think it was the latter part of 1946. I took over the editorship of *Mullai*, a monthly magazine run by my friend P. Muthiah. Pudumaipithan and I were talking to each other daily. One day, he asked me a question all of a sudden.

'If I write *Kutrala Kuravanji* into a film script, will it work? What do you think?'

'Has anyone asked you? If it works or not, it is okay if we get money,' I said.

'It is not for anyone else. It is my production.'

I could not respond to him. I was very close to him and knew almost every secret of his. When he spoke of his production, I could not come to terms with it.

'Why are you rolling your eyes? Something good will happen,' he said, nodding.

Pudumaipithan did not have money to make a film. There is no way a huge amount of money would come and land on him. Pudumaipithan could not even bargain for material worth five rupees. How could he deal with a production worthy of five lakh rupees? It was going to be a disaster if he tried to deal with such huge productions.

I never got to know the secrets of the birth of Parvathakumari Productions. I never knew its intimate details either. Pudumaipithan's literary friends Ki. Ramachandran and Loganathan did not know about the film production company. We don't know if he concealed the information on his own accord, or at the behest of someone else. You cannot hide either the dregs of the gutter or incense. Both are given away by their smell. We could sense what was happening with the Parvathakumari Productions.

Many people entering films as actors, camerapersons, or script writers, want to produce their own films. This desire is the result of either a love for art or a love for money. Some of them pursue it and are successful at it. For some, it remains an unfulfilled dream. Pudumaipithan's entry into films expanded his sphere of influence. It added some unique friends to his circle. They surrounded him all the time. The new friends added Pudumaipithan to their circle of influential acquaintances and used his name to get ahead in their careers. Pudumaipithan was thus ensnared, and lost his poise.

A Tamil proverb says that the beggars come together to build a religious mutt. When the beggars seek alms, they don't cling together. Each one goes his way. If Parvathakumari Productions became a mutt of the beggars, it was no surprise. Pudumaipithan's determination to create a base of his own took a toll on him. Pudumaipithan and his coterie traveled to Secunderabad, Tirunelveli, and Trivandrum, in search of capital. Pudumaipithan's savings were exhausted in this venture. There was no sign of hope for the film production company. It was a pure waste of the hard-earned wealth of Pudumaipithan.

One of my friends used to tell me this, 'Even the germs of plague leave the person after he is dead. Some people are worse than that. They suck the person's blood when he is alive and don't even leave him after he is gone.' The circle of film friends of Pudumaipithan behaved worse than plague germs. Even when Pudumaipithan was down and out, they encircled him and made use of him. They told him that if they advertised the film, someone would believe them and invest money in them. Pudumaipithan agreed. Some newspapers carried the advertisement. The advertisement carried the name of Parvathakumari Productions and the name of the film hero – Nagercoil Mahadevan.

I remember with sadness one incident that happened just before the release of the advertisement. I think it was the festive season of Deepavali. Pudumaipithan wanted to go home. He did not have money. He had to take the night train to get home. He had one and a quarter anna with him. Nagercoil Mahadevan and coterie were present at Pudumaipithan's house. I was also there. 'It won't be appropriate to publish the name of Nagercoil Mahadevan without paying him in advance,' said Pudumaipithan. One member of the coterie extended a currency note to him. 'Producer' Pudumaipithan handed over the currency note to Nagercoil Mahadevan. The contract came into force with immediate effect. They deliberated on Pudumaipithan's wish to visit home during Deepavali. By four o'clock in the afternoon, the team borrowed 100 Rupees from somewhere. In an hour, Pudumaipithan had only less than ten rupees. The fruits for the family, the taxi fare to reach the railway station took about fifteen rupees. I can understand these expenses. His train fare was seventy-five rupees. It was a first-class ticket. Because he was a film producer.

There were many such occasions. When money was wasted like water. I am full of sadness and laughter when I think of such occasions.

'It looks like you cannot survive on the planet by practicing your profession,' God tells Kandasamy Pillai, in one of the short stories by Pudumaipithan. Pudumaipithan may have thrived if he had only practiced his profession. 'We can barely survive by practicing our profession. We cannot survive with something we don't know.' This was the lesson Pudumaipithan had to learn from his experience of running Parvathakumari Productions, a daydream.

Pune

The bigoted communalist Godse shot Mahatma Gandhi dead on 30th January 1948. That bigot was from the city of Pune. He was running a magazine from Pune. Pudumaipithan wrote a letter to a friend K.T. Thevar in Mumbai. K.T. Thevar is a Tamil enthusiast. He is now in Coimbatore as part of *Sakthi* magazine. During his stay in Pune, Pudumaipithan developed a good rapport with Thevar. The following is part of what Pudumaipithan wrote to Thevar:

> '... before Mahatma's body could be burned, Pune is burning. Pune is a distortion of Punya (virtue). It took so long to understand its real meaning. We name the completely blind person as Nallakannu Pillai (good-eyed person). This city has ended up on the wrong side of history. I don't feel like living in this city...'

Just because it gave birth to the killer of Mahatma Gandhi, the city of virtue became the city of sin. Pudumaipithan was completely upset. Pune did not just give birth to the killer of Mahatma. The city also aggravated the tuberculosis in Pudumaipithan. Tuberculosis eventually ate away at the creative genius that was Pudumaipithan.

When Pudumaipithan lived in Chennai, he was not coughing so much. When he was at the Royapettah High Road residence in Chennai, he used to cough his lungs out at times. He did not suspect it was tuberculosis. He believed in the Siddha system of medicine. He said that he had done the examination. He said that it was only asthma. He did not have that cough regularly. He had it only when he got exhausted or when he had smoked a lot. He used to cough until his eyes were filled with water. No one doubted that it might be tuberculosis. But there were no other explicit symptoms of the disease.

Had Pudumaipithan taken care of his body then, he could have avoided falling prey to the deadly tuberculosis. He did not pay enough attention to his health. He only took Chyawanprash, an indigenous medication for cough, and some English medicines to keep his cough under control. He never opted for a holistic treatment of the symptoms. Also, the burden associated with Parvathakumari Productions, as mentioned in the last chapter, added to his woes. His was a very weak body. It was vulnerable to communicable diseases like tuberculosis. If Pudumaipithan had good food, good sleep, and good rest, the disease may not have touched him. Parvathakumari Productions depleted his savings. He had to struggle for a meal. He starved many times. His sense of pride did not allow him to borrow money. He had the avatar of a film producer. He had to travel from city to city in search of the capital that would justify that role. The vain efforts led to his frustration, sleeplessness, and exhaustion. The production company never paid off. It led to his ill-health.

Pudumaipithan's health deteriorated when he stayed in Pune for work. The disease dominated him. He worked tirelessly in Pune. There was no one to take care of him. There was no healthy food. The dormant tuberculosis, hidden away in his body, started wreaking havoc. He continued to work hard, knowing well that he would not live much longer. The disease spread across his body before he could finish scripting *Rajamukthi*. Pudumaipithan had to return to his home due to illness.

The letters written by Pudumaipithan during his stay in Pune are evidence of the deadly tuberculosis he lived with. His friends or relatives could not witness his experiences with TB in Pune. The letters are the only proof.

In a letter written to wife Kamalambal on his arrival in Pune, he explained his difficulties. He continued to inform her about the progress of the disease. The following extracts are from the letters he has written to his wife. The letters describe the pain of the disease.

> Date: 07th November 1947
>
> '...Pune City: I cannot explain the struggles I am going through here. There is a change of place every day. Marathi Brahmin food. God alone should appreciate it. There is no facility for taking a bath. It is two days since I got here. Some construction work is underway. They are building a toilet. I have enough food. But my body is weakening. The swelling and pain in my hand remain. No cure. There is no use describing each of my pains to you...'

> Date: 20th December 1947
>
> '...You cannot think worse about me than the way I think about myself. There is a reason why I could not respond to your recent letter. I was afraid of

myself. I did not want to intimidate you. I got perplexed as to how to deal with the situation. I hesitated to reveal my disease. It is T.B.'

Date: 04th January 1948

'...I am not satisfied with the conclusion of one doctor on my disease. I am planning to meet two more doctors. I am waiting for the final results. Some doctors may misdiagnose the disease. I am meeting an X-ray doctor here. I am also consulting with a famous Ayurvedic doctor here. The body has become so weak. I sit in one place and keep working. Not moving about. The cough has reduced because of an on-going medication. Breathlessness is common. Fruits, milk, Horlicks, and rice are the usual diet. They advised me to have a bath after applying fish oil to the body. I am starting on it tomorrow. I don't like eggs. I have to find a substitute for it. I should eat very healthy food. The doctor has advised me to keep constipation away. The frequent fever has subsided for the last two days. Sinhagad is a forest near this place. The fountain water there is a medicine for

T.B. They sell it here. I have made arrangements to obtain it after the doctor's advice. If I am a bit alright, we can go and stay in Sinhagad...

...Weakness of the body is causing difficulty. It would be good to have hair oil. I don't get it here. I want to take care of myself. You don't have to fear or worry. You are upset because the child is asking for me, with her own words. It would be painful for you to go through this – a thousand miles away from me...'

Date: 24th January 1948

'...I don't have the strength in my hand to write a long letter. I had a 102-degree fever for three days. And cough. I will get the X-ray sheet and the doctor's opinion this evening. I will also consult other doctors to ascertain it is T.B. I need someone to take care of me. I don't like to drag you into this. You are taking care of the child. You should not come to me...'

Date: 26th January 1948

'...Sputum has piled up in the body. It is a communicable disease. Doctors advised me to use a mask while speaking and to use separate utensils. I should not wander around. I should limit my work. That is what doctors tell me. After my return from the doctors' I had a fever of 103 degrees. Recurring fever is a characteristic of this disease…'

Date: February 5, 1948
'…I did not get betel leaves for four days. Think of my situation. I got a fever today. I am writing this with a 102-degree fever. I am planning to come by the month-end. You will realize the graveness of my situation on seeing me…'

Date: February 9, 1948
'…Gandhi was assassinated. I could not venture out for three days because a curfew was in place. There is a hotel near the studio. Six miles is the distance between them. Public movement is not allowed. I carry medicines, thermometers, and shawls at the cost of provoking some ridicule. I exhausted the medicines. Shops are shuttered until the last rites of Mahatma Gandhi. The city is burning and I cannot venture out. I

am peaceful today as I don't have a fever. The doctor who is treating me now, is brilliant. His medicine has put an end to my fever. If I take bed rest for three months, the disease can be cured. He asks me not to speak. I will be cured. Do not fear. Do not disturb yourself by imagining bad things about my condition...'

Date: April 8, 1948
'...my health has become worse. That is why all the plans have failed. If I get better after coming home, you are fortunate...'

We can hear the pain of Pudumaipithan from the lines written by him. The disease had aggravated by the day. That is why he decided to go home. The disease was already dominant at the beginning of 1948. It grew worse in three months. The condition deteriorated in April. That was when he decided to go home. His wife received a telegram that said that he would be home by May 5, 1948.

The sacred land of Pune did not want to bear the sin of witnessing his last days. It packed him off to Thiruvananthapuram to spend his twilight days.

Twilight Days

'Pudumaipithan is lucky. He got a chance to write for Bagavathar. He does not have to worry about the future,' is how other writers perceived his situation at that time.

'We heard that Bagavathar gave you ten thousand rupees. Please invest the money in some land,' his uncle wrote to him.

'He would have given the money to his wife's home by now. He will not invest in land or home,' said some of his relatives.

When Pudmaipithan landed at Thiruvananthapuram railway station in the first week of May 1948, all he had was tuberculosis. Many people may not understand what led to such a situation. I don't want to explain the situation. One letter may tell us the reality of Pudumaipithan circumstances then. Raja Ariyaratnam is the editor of *Eelakesari*, published from Jaffna in Sri Lanka. He is a patron of Tamil literary personalities. Pudumaipithan wrote a letter to him in his last days:

> Date: June 17, 1948
> '...It has been tough for me in the last two years. When I was weak, the disease entered the body. I became bedridden. I was in Pune to write the film of Bagavathar. My financial situation has become pretty bad. Can the writers and readers of Jaffna fund me to fight the disease? Think about it and respond to me as soon as possible...'

He had also written to Kana. Muthiah of Tamil Puthakalayam in Chennai in the middle of May. 'Even a small amount will be of great help at this moment,' is what he said in the postcard.

S.Chidambaram,afriendfromThiruvananthapuram, came to see me on June 26, 1948. I was in Tirunelveli. He brought a message from Pudumaipithan.

> 'The service I have done to Tamil Nadu is irrefutable. I am on my deathbed now. I am here because of poverty. I have the right to ask

> for help from the people of Tamil Nadu. Please consult other writers, publicize my situation in the newspapers, and seek help. I can write about my condition if you wish...'

This was the message from him.

He has written many short stories, essays, and poems. But he could not write a single line during his last days. He was so weak that he had to dictate the letters to someone else and then sign them. These letters are proof of his deteriorating health and poor financial situation.

As soon as Pudumaipithan reached Thiruvananthapuram, his wife, daughter, and relatives were by his side. Chidambaram, his friend from Thiruvananthapuram, was by his side until his last breath. It depends on the observer, to see this last meeting as a boon or a bane. Thiruvananthapuram Chidambaram had great regard for Pudumaipithan. He is interested in the new wave of modern literature. He published *Kavikkuyil*, a literary special edition, for two years. He has been writing as well. The information shared by him and Pudumaipithan's wife about the last days of the literary giant is disturbing and unsettles me.

Pudumaipithan was always thin. His physique was quite like a stick. Tuberculosis – known for eating away one's flesh – devastated him. The ribs were visible. It is as if he had just skin enough to cover his bones. There was no flesh. He had grown a beard and looked a bit awkward. His continuous cough discharged sputum and blood. And there was a recurring fever.

Pudumaipithan came home. He needed a walking stick to get off the train. He had to be supported to reach home. He did not have the energy to answer the people around him. He could barely move his lips. The words could not reach the listeners. He had a cup of coffee as soon as he reached home. 'I got good coffee only today.' Then he went silent.

Chidambaram went to see him the next day. Shocked by the condition of Pudumaipithan, he asked him, 'When you are so weak, how could you travel such a long distance?'

Pudumaipithan smiled and said, 'I came prepared for any eventuality. It is about desire. Her memories [i.e. Dinakari's] brought me here.' He caressed Dinakari's hair for a while. 'I do things out of emotion. I don't realize their consequences. Then live with the repercussions. Is that right?'

Pudumaipithan was hopeless about his condition when he arrived in Thiruvananthapuram. But his family members wanted to cure him somehow. They took him to the doctor. 'The disease has reached a terminal stage. Go see a doctor in Nagercoil.' Some people advised that it would help if he was taken to Bengaluru. The doctor in Bengaluru advised that there was no cure at this point. He suggested that Pudumaipithan return to Thiruvananthapuram and take rest. Pudumaipithan was back in Thiruvananthapuram.

Pudumaipithan realized that death was near. He thought of Jack London's story 'Love of Life,' which he had translated. It is easy to die. It is hard to live. It is natural to want to live. Pudumaipithan also wanted to live. He started Ayurvedic treatment for the condition.

Chidambaram visited Pudumaipithan often. One day he saw a powder being readied for Pudumaipithan's treatment.

'Chidambaram, don't be surprised that TB has Ayurvedic treatment. The Bengaluru doctor said he could not treat me. The local doctor here also said he could not treat me. So finally we have this treatment,' said Pudumaipithan with a smile.

'Do you know Minjirai, Chidambaram? Minjirai is not a treatise. It is a town. A doctor in this town is treating me,' said Pudumaipithan.

Pudumaipithan, in his last days, spoke of his life with mixed feelings. He spoke of his days in Pune. 'The world is a strange place. People don't give you money when you are healthy. Imagine the situation when you are sick. They fear that you would run away with money. You are respected only until you have not fallen sick. I am sick. But I had talent.'

His journey to Pune was in search of better fortunes. The city gave him some harsh experiences. His pain lasted until his last breath. But he spoke with a bit of satire. This shows his determination and passion. He had engaging conversations until his last moment.

'How is the literary world? I cannot read and find out. Please tell me. I am curious,' said Pudumaipithan.

Chidambaram explained in detail what the scenario was. Pudumaipithan listened and finally said this: 'Chidambaram, I know that you are passionate about literature. That is ok. But do not spend all your time in literature. If you choose literature as a profession, it can kill you. Literature will only bring you penury. Keep it as your pastime.'

Pudumaipithan spoke of literature on the eve of his death: 'Is literature alive? It will always be alive. It does not stop because I am dying. When I die, all my well-wishers will write obituaries and remember me. In a matter of days, people will forget the incident...'

He was overwhelmed with memories. Though Chidambaram and relatives sat by his side, it looked as if he spoke to himself: 'I was born somewhere, I was raised somewhere, so many people brought me up, it looks like my last breath will be in Thiruvananthapuram...'

Pudumaipithan was dying. He has written a short story on a Muslim beggar dying on Mount Road (Anna Salai) in Chennai. There was no one to take care of that person when he was dying. Literary personalities did not care about what happened to their fellow writer. In his loneliness, Pudumaipithan was dying day by day.

We may think that he would have loved some monetary help from the well-wishers during the last few days. He was in a different mindset during the last hours of his life.

'The arrival of a money order will make me happy. I am expecting a money order now. Don't you get it? I look forward to death as if I expect a money order,' said Pudumaipithan.

On the eve of his death, Pudumaipithan asked Chidambaram to replace the batteries in his torchlight. 'Writers always love light. I wanted to brighten all the paths I trod. Now, I am asking for light to guide me in darkness.'

He wanted the torchlight to walk into the darkness of his home. The darkness of death had already enveloped him. There is no escape from that darkness. He was waiting to die in the darkness. Pudumaipithan who illuminated the world through his writing was not afraid of dying in the darkness. He welcomed death with a smile. He only worried that his death should not intimidate others.

It was the last day of his life. It was June 30, 1948. The people who stayed in Pudumaipithan's home that day could smell the coming death. They feared the moment.

Moment by moment, Pudumaipithan was dying.

He was sweating profusely. Kamalambal was wiping it. Others watched. Pudumaipithan started talking, saying 'Kamala, I am leaving behind the *Rajamukthi* film and Dinakari. Don't worry. I wanted to take good care of you. But destiny has brought me to this situation.'

After the night of June 30, 1948, the whole world woke up. Pudumaipithan did not wake up. Pudumaipithan was no more…

His wife and relatives cried, shouted, and lamented….

They did not say:

> 'The immortal one has descended from the sky;
> He returned as he came.'

'Your hands have swollen because you kept writing. You sacrificed your life as well,' is how Kamalambal lamented.

That cry reverberated across the house.

The King of Short Stories is Dead

> Today is the death anniversary of Kamban; Poems
> Reached the throne on this day. Today is
> When in the presence of the Goddess of Land and
> the Goddess of Wealth,
> The Goddess of Tongue removes the sacred thread!

It is what a poet wrote when the great poet Kambar died. Pudumaipithan once argued with me to say that Kambar himself authored this poem. Kambar alone dared to say that Goddess Saraswati could lose her sacred thread. That was Pudumaipithan's argument. 'Kambar must have been upset that his genius did not get appropriate recognition. He would have seen mediocre writers getting undue recognition. That is the reason he kept this ready when he was alive.' This was how Pudumaipithan justified Kambar's authorship of these lines.

Pudumaipithan got an opportunity to prove this in public. In 1946, the Tiruchi station of All India Radio invited him to give a talk. 'How do songs originate?' is the topic of the talk. He prepared a talk. He mentioned this idea of Kambar writing about his death when he was alive. He explained why Kambar was upset about many things in the literary world. He demonstrated how the sense of being wronged could lead to a flow of creative energy in the writer.

What if Pudumaipithan had died before he could deliver the address to All India Radio? He said the literary rivals would celebrate such a moment with great happiness. 'Has he gone?' They would heave a sigh of relief. The literary quacks who were afraid of Pudumaipithan would be very happy. They would celebrate his demise. He, in turn, would respond to them with a song:

> He said he would go to Tiruchi. But he has gone forever.
> Have you heard the sound of the train? – the bald
> Fool! The inefficient fool!
> The beggar fool! Leave now!

It is jealousy. It is rivalry. It is the sound of anger that you hear in the song.

Pudumaipithan could not go to Tiruchi on the day of the appointment. His talk could not be broadcast.

Pudumaipithan did not go to Tiruchi. He went to Thiruvananthapuram in the last days of his life. He left all of us from there. He remained the king of Tamil short stories until his last breath. He said goodbye to all of us on the midnight of June 30, 1948.

Family and Child

'...Bramma Nayakam Pillai has seen the ups and downs of life. Every up has a down. He started his life on a higher plane.'

Pudumaipithan had a similar experience to Bramma Nayakam Pillai after he left his home in Tirunelveli. There was no guarantee of a good life. The challenges of financial security and a hopelessly scarce income continued to bother him. His family life had the same difficulties as a middle-class family.

'The person marrying a writer should be an adventurer,' said one of my friends. I don't know about the writers of other countries. If a woman is marrying a writer in Tamil Nadu, she should be a courageous one. Though we have a rhetoric about 'Our Tamil! Our Tamil!' the people who can appreciate good writing are in small numbers. It is hard to sustain a livelihood on writing. We cannot dismiss it as something about writing alone. The entire middle class is going through such a tough challenge. Social reforms will democratize education further. That will lead to an appreciation of art and literature. When reforms are complete, writing can be a full-time profession like any other job.

When Kamalambal married Pudumaipithan, there was no space for this conversation. Pudumaipithan was a graduate with a B.A. degree, and the son of Chockalingam Pillai, a *tehsildar.* He was the eldest son from a decent family. There is no way Kamalambal knew that he was a writer. She may not have anticipated that she would also start writing stories in the future.

Ramakrishna Pillai built the 'Ramakrishna House' in Thiruvananthapuram. Kamalambal was born here as the daughter of Subramania Pillai. Kamala's father is no more. She has brothers and sisters. Her brothers did not give her comfort. They fought the family elders in the court to get their share of wealth. Pudumaipithan's father told me that his son was influenced by the practices of his in-law's family. Kamala did not enjoy great peace back home. 'I did not see love in my home,' was Pudumaipithan's complaint. Kamalambal had a similar situation. Pudumaipithan had emotional support from Kamalambal. 'Kamala, whatever earnings I may have, if you were not by my side, I would have become a street beggar,' he told his wife. Though Kamalambal lived with him, she found it challenging to understand him. His readers found it difficult to comprehend his stories.

'I tried to understand him since we came together. I tried to change his behavior. I exhorted him to trust and love life. I could not convince him. I don't know if the life we lived together was one of happiness or sadness. I am not sure about it,' said Kamalambal.

Kamalambal faced a lot of difficulties throughout her lifetime. She was not happy when she lived with him. She has faced a difficult future after his leaving. 'I was born into a good family. I got married into a good family. Both are decent families. He and I faced disappointments, failures, and difficulties together,' said Kamalambal.

Kamalambal had endured a hostile family situation because of her brothers. Pudumaipithan could not experience love at home because of his stepmother. They came to Chennai and struggled to make a decent living. By now, you know the entire story.

In the short story 'Chithi,' Pudumaipithan describes the role of a wife:

'In a family, only one person can know how the man is conducting himself. The person who steps onto a grindstone, during the wedding rites, and looks at the

Arundhati star with you, with the world as your witness. She alone, who steps into your life, will understand how the relationship is shaping up and progressing. The wise will know. Those who don't have the option of knowing about it will have an incomplete idea of how the bond is developing.'

Going by this formula of understanding the health of family life, the only person who can tell the world about it, is Kamalambal. She says, 'I could not understand him.' I was away from him when he was in the thick of his family life. I am not the person to talk about the health of Pudumaipithan's family life. I am not the authority on that aspect of the writer's life. Let us leave it at that.

However, we have some written evidence of the love displayed between the couple. In an essay, Kamalambal says the following about love life:

> 'I don't realize how time passes when he is speaking to me. He will come with betel leaves and sit down in the kitchen. Sometimes, he will be waiting for friends. He will ask me to tell them that he is not home. I will open the door and tell them that he is not in. He will

tell them from inside, "I am in," and make me feel ashamed…

He will buy me books that are easy to read. He will make me like whatever he likes. He never considers his wife as a slave who is ready to serve him. I experienced so much freedom with him. He never treated me as inferior or different from him. I am always his equal. He spends generously when he has money. He does not worry if he does not have money. I could not tolerate such a mind-set. I admonish him for being irresponsible. He will ask me not to worry too much. He will also promise that the next day will be very good…

I realized that he could not manage money very well. I started taking responsibility. He will hand over the salary to me. Whenever there is a need, he will ask me for money.

He will not hesitate to display his love and affection for me in front of others. Some relatives will complain about it. They ask, what is it that he finds so attractive in me?

His father once wrote to him. "You are giving your wife so much freedom. This is

> injurious to our Hindu tradition and customs."
> I felt so much pain in reading this.
>
> "Why is he writing like this? I don't understand," I asked.
>
> He clarified to me that they don't like him being open and free with me. He asked me not to worry about it. He comforted me. He does not stop with that. He wrote back to his father. In the letter, he said: "Your opinion is relevant only in the case of a young woman marrying an older man. I have not done that. I have not done a ritual wedding." When he feels that someone is not doing it right, he will respond with frankness like this. That is his habit.'

Pudumaipithan was working in *Dinamani*. Kamalambal was at her parents' place. Pudumaipithan had promised to take her to Chennai once he found a house. He found a house. Maybe he did not want her to struggle with him in Chennai. He wrote to her saying 'I have not found a home. You don't have to come now.' Kamalambal could not live without him. She did not wait for his consent. 'I am coming. Meet me at the station' was the telegraph message she sent him. She landed at the Egmore railway station the next morning with all the utensils to start a new home. She did not find Pudumaipithan at the station.

She took a taxi and reached the office of *Dinamani* by 8 am. She did not have the details of the place where he was residing. The taxi left, leaving her behind with the luggage. The office would open only at 10 am. She was on the street. The office boy arrived first. The door was opened. The message could not be passed on despite some efforts.

Pudumaipithan arrived at the office at 10 am.

'You left me in the street. Is this my destiny?' asked Kamalambal.

'You could have sent a telegraph message,' he said.

'I sent it,' she said.

They realized that the telegraph did not arrive on time. Pudumaipithan was angry that his wife was not welcomed into the office. He later realized that it was his fault that she had to endure this.

Pudumaipithan and Kamalambal lived as husband and wife for almost fifteen years. Kamalambal had to go to her parental home in Thiruvananthapuram for childbirth and rest. He would not bring her back to Chennai easily. He never wanted her to partake in the difficulties he was facing. Even when she is upset and angry, Pudumaipithan would make her smile. The following letter is an example of that. He wrote this to her in 1943.

> '...I got the letter you posted without a stamp yesterday. If I miss the instalment, am I the culprit? If the employer gives the money, it will not even wait a second and will come flying to you. You are still behaving like a child and are good at fighting with me. When the letter arrived, it was almost time for the money to arrive. I wanted to send the letter along with the money. In the meantime, you bombarded me with a stamp-less letter. When I got the letter, my colleagues in the office laughed thinking that we fought. I also laughed. I did not get angry. The letter only brought a smile to my face. You will chase away the opponent when you are angry. Then you will feel bad that you chased away the person. I am deeply aware of your habits. You are mistaking my patience for lethargy. Then you get angry at me. You are getting upset with me. Old stories get exaggerated in your mind. You pick up the pen

and pour all the anger out in the paper. I am thinking of your face now. It looks as if you've swerved when someone tries to hit you in anger. Don't have suspicions like a little child. What else can I say? I feel like kissing you and saying baby, baby. You think that me not writing a letter for some time is a crime. When I arrange money, people ask for more time. I am disappointed each time it gets delayed. If I keep writing about such delays, it will add to your disappointment. You will say that my word is not worth trusting. If I don't send money and write a letter, you will feel bad again. You will say that you have written to me about the need for money. I understand your feelings. If I was in your position, I would also feel angry about the situation. When people ask for more time to give money, I also feel angry. You are free to express your anger. I don't have that luxury. I have to have the patience. You are becoming more like a child day by day. Whatever the amount of anger you may have, I would like to see a moment when your anger is gone. It is like hugging and kissing a baby tight when she

> is throwing her legs and spitting on me. Your anger is for the moment. It will disappear after that moment…'

Pudumaipithan liked children. His love for and interest in children were incredible. We can fairly understand his love for children from the child characters he created in the short stories 'Chittannai' and 'Kadavulum Kandasamy Pillayum.' Pudumaipithan was like Periyazhwar, the Vaishnavite Saint who used his *Pasurams* (hymns) to celebrate the praise of Baby Krishna. Pudumaipithan celebrated many children through his stories. He left behind Dinakari, a girl child. His other children – a boy and a girl – died in childhood.

When his first child died, he could not travel to his hometown. Financial crunch. He once told me about this. That was the time Pudumaipithan's stories were out. His publisher approached him and sought help. He explained his financial situation and asked for the rights of one of Pudumaipithan's titles. Pudumaipithan agreed and signed the contract for it. The publisher came back to Pudumaipithan to ask for money. Pudumaipithan got angry.

He responded to him like this:

I killed my child because of you.
I killed my book for you.
I cannot kill myself for you.

Dinakari was born on the first day of Chithirai, the first month in the Tamil calendar. That was the year 1946. I was with him when he received the telegram 'Baby born.' He was ecstatic. He bought toys, balls, and other items, and left the same night to see the child. He had wanted this childbirth to be natural. He was happy, yet anxious about the health of the mother and child. Pudumaipithan reached Thiruvananthapuram and saw the mother and the child. He wrote a letter to me from there.

> '...I wish to write a long letter. But my body is not cooperating. I am thinking of you when I am having food. Though we are such good friends, we have different stomachs. I am against Communist idealism since last night. In the communist system, we don't have space for the house of in-laws. For those who journey long distances, a meal and hot water feel like nectar.

> Only the mother-in-law can provide that with care. If the mother is doing the same, the son will be spoilt. He will become useless. Mother's love can remove your worries. A mother-in-law's care and affection remove your bodily pain and make the world a better place. ... If I keep telling stories and not coming to the important message of the day, you will get angry. Contrary to my fears, it was a natural delivery. The child is healthy. She is making a lot of noise here. I have left the hospital and reached home. After you, the child captivates my imagination now...'

Pudumaipithan had great affection for his daughter Dinakari. When he was struggling with tuberculosis in Pune, he wrote many letters to his wife. Some of the letters bear evidence of his love for Dinakari. I am quoting some portions here:

> 'Here is nothing serious about me. You don't have to keep worrying about it. Take care of Dinakari. Keep the thoughts about great destiny to ourselves. Take care of Dinakari's health. I have kept the goods bought for her

> under the cot. I am sending them tomorrow. I am also planning to buy more toys…'
>
> '….your blind love for me is not an intelligent idea. If you wish to be by my side, think of the child. My survival or death is dependent on destiny. How can we be irresponsible and pass on a communicable disease to an innocent child? Think about it. Love should be accompanied by intelligence. Otherwise, it will be a disaster…'
>
> 'My flying kisses to Dinakari on this New Year. I never thought she had to go through this…'
>
> 'Is Dinakari baby searching for me? Are you taking her out in the evening? Or are you leaving her to cry? She is in my mind's eye every moment. My worries will go away if you visit me…'

The reason Pudumaipithan came back to Thiruvananthapuram was to see Dinakari. Despite the serious illness, he made an effort and came back to see her. His love for Dinakari was incredible. That is why he gave his mother's name, Parvatha Kumari, as the second name to her. When he felt that he had a great beginning in films, Dinakari was born. He also named his film venture after Parvatha Kumari.

Pudumaipithan's love for children is not the only reason he showered affection on Dinakari. He did not get an opportunity to spend quality time with his children who died young. In the story 'Kadavulum Kandasamy Pillaiyum,' the protagonist introduces a child to God. 'She is like a *karuveppilai kozhunthu* (budding curry leaf) for our desire.' Dinakari is that one exceptional being. Pudumaipithan thought she would be the last and only daughter to him. 'She is like the last dosa that we make. We increase the dough with water and make a last dosa. My other children passed away. She is the last one to come. That is why I made that analogy,' he once told a friend. The friend asked about her age. 'She does not have an age. Looking at her intelligence, she should be my mother's age,' said a proud and beaming Pudumaipithan.

Dinakari lived on to be the one and only heir of Pudumaipithan. Yama, the God of Death, took him away in the second year of Dinakari's birth.

Chovi

Many readers know Pudumaipithan only through his stories. Many don't know what he looked like. They may not know have known what sort of a person he was. They may have felt his heart in his stories. They may wish to know how he appeared and interacted with others in real life. I had the same wish years ago. I understand why people wish to have some knowledge of the daily life of their favourite author. In this section, I am trying to bring alive the character that was Pudumaipithan.

Imagine this, Pudumaipithan is of reasonable height. He is about 5.75 feet high. He does not have flesh proportionate to his height. A thin physique. The loose white khadi *jippa* (a large shirt) conceals his thinness. He will have a lot of hair and bundle it to the back of the head. The hair will be dishevelled in no time. His hair is not unruly. He just keeps pushing it to the back of the head. The hair will remain loose as he keeps adjusting it often. There will be silver streaks here and there in his hair. His forehead is broader. Just as an uncultivable land is full of broken lines, his forehead has wrinkles. As pearls from underneath the ocean radiate brightness, his eyes from emit light from deep within. You see some craziness in the eyes. It is craziness with a kind of yearning. It gives an illusion of age. We can call them 'Boris Karloff' eyes. If you wish to know what it is, look at the cover of Pudumaipithan's book of translations, *Pretha Manithan*. But imagine an added amount of light. You can see insatiable yearning, craziness, light, and clarity in the eyes. You can look into the eyes of some people endlessly. But you cannot look into Pudumaipithan's eyes like that. They will repulse you quite soon. His nose is straight, and a bit protruding. His teeth are on the bigger side. You cannot see the reddish effect of betel leaves there. But they are yellowish. 'Mango leaves oscillate unevenly, like my teeth' is a description he uses in the story 'Vinayaka Chathurthi.' You should not believe it. They are indeed big like mango leaves. But they are not uneven. His lips are bigger. His lower lip is bulging. His continuous use of betel leaves made the lower lip harder. You can almost always see his front-row teeth. His chest has no flesh. It looks like a set of bones covered in skin. His hands and legs are thin. He looks older because of his weak-looking body. He keeps nodding his head while speaking. He does not stop nodding even when others speak. He keeps nodding. He keeps adjusting his hair. He always smiles. He keeps chewing betel leaves. He looks up and laughs loudly. It is an innocent smile. For those who are new to him, it can be annoying or disgusting. He laughs without any filter. It may even look barbaric to highly sophisticated people. The laugh is not just a sign of happiness. It is a way of measuring the intelligence of the person having a conversation with him. Sometimes, it is a moment's respite, so that he can think of an intelligent response to the question that was posed.

He is always engaged in some kind of talk. Even when he has too many commitments in writing, he will never cease talking. His talking gets interrupted by a cough sometimes. He will have some water after the cough. He will have betel leaves. He will talk again. It was a pleasure talking to him. We will also start laughing with him. His subjects for conversation are unlimited. Ancient literature, modern literature, music, astrology, Siddha medicine, the songs of Siddhar, *Thirumanthiram*, *Kambaramayanam*, literature on lust, gossip, and current affairs form part of his conversation. I still remember him explaining to me Einstein's Theory of Relativity to me. I am not sure if he knows everything about these subjects. He is quite assertive while talking. When he talks about medicine and astrology, it appears as if he has an in depth knowledge and belief in those systems. He wanted to write a novel based on a protagonist's horoscope. He decided the life events of a protagonist. He asked an astrologer to assign an astrological chart to the character. People who have seen such incidents believe that he has strong beliefs in astrology and traditional medicine. People who are close to him, like me, do not know if he believed in astrology or traditional medicine.

It is better to let him speak, and listen to him. If someone interrupts he will stop speaking. He is not upset about such interruptions. He will listen to such interruptions carefully. Once the person who interrupted completes talking, Pudumaipithan will not go back to the subject he was talking about. He does not like going back to the subject after a break. Even if someone reminds him of the incomplete talk, he would love to abandon it. Many people want to showcase their intelligence by interfering in a conversation. It may be off-putting for him. He never expressed it. Only a few people know about this habit of Pudumaipithan. Whenever he speaks on a subject, he reveals rare truths. His genius and satire are on display.

He uses English words in his talk. His Tamil has an authentic Tirunelveli pronunciation. Those who migrated to Chennai will usually acquire some inflections from Madrasi Tamil, over the years. Pudumaipithan maintained the sounds of Tirunelveli Tamil in his speech until his last days. 'Rasa,' 'Avuha,' 'Vanthaha,' 'Mesai' are some of the Tirunelveli sounds he maintained. 'Adikkadi,' 'Vivaharam,' 'Irukku,' and 'Position' are some of the words repeated by him during conversations.

His gait is unique. He walks slowly. He leans forward and limps a little bit like a goat confronting another goat. He folds his dhoti above his knee and walks on the road like a true blue Tirunelveli person. If he sees a friend on the way he smiles generously and folds his hands to give respect. He has a certain posture while sitting, wherever he goes. If he is sitting on a mat at home or sitting in an office chair or a chair in a friend's home, he sits cross-legged. For him, the floor and the chair are the same.

He wakes up early in the morning, even if he goes to bed late. On alternate days, he shaves. He spends about half an hour brushing his teeth. He uses toothpaste or *Karuvelam* tooth powder, a traditional variety. He will try his best to get rid of the reddish stain developed by the constant use of betel leaves. He uses a coconut leaf stick to clean his tongue. It will lead to a loud cough. It will fill his eyes with tears. He does not give up. This morning routine is a must for him. He will use some herb-based hair oil generously. He will oil his hands and legs as well. During the bath, he uses *peerkangai* and *shikakai* (soap nut powder) along with the soap. After the bath, he chews betel leaves. Morning coffee is only after this ritual.

He is careful about hygiene. He will do everything to keep his body and clothes clean. He won't entertain those who don't take a bath and have uncombed hair. He will avoid patients. He is afraid of people with communicable diseases. He will run away from them. A writer with a communicable disease kept visiting him at home often. Pudumaipithan would fume inside when he was sitting on the cot or chair. He could not express his displeasure because he was a fellow writer. He would discard the tumbler that was used to give the writer water or coffee. He used the sanitizer and cleaned up the entire room after the writer had left. He feared communicable diseases so much. He hated communicable diseases. He cared so much about cleanliness. He cared for hygiene. It is an irony he had to die of a communicable disease called tuberculosis.

Pudumaipithan loved talking. His love for talking supersedes his love for food. His love for betel leaves is even bigger than that. If he has a companion for conversation, coffee, and betel leaves, he does not need food. If someone asks 'Don't want to eat?' his response is: 'Oh! We have that duty left!' He might then get up to eat. Sometimes, he continues the conversation. All he wants is two morsels of food. He is particular about taste. He will walk a considerable distance to make sure that he gets quality food. He always loves a good coffee. He will not drink coffee at any shop. 'You want to drink coffee here? He boils water and calls it coffee,' is a remark he once made. He only likes strong coffee with less sugar. He loves coffee with its aroma.

The habit of chewing betel leaves started at a very young age. He smokes a cigarette or a cigar occasionally. He did not have a craving for cigarettes. He loved costly and high-quality tobacco products. I once told him that I had seen a 999 cigarette in a shop on Broadway. He sent an assistant to that shop immediately to get that brand of cigarette. The boy got only one 999 cigarette. He gave that to me saying, 'You should not be disappointed.' Cigarettes are never a part of his routine. He is not addicted to cigarettes. But chewing betel leaves is his routine and a habit.

In the short story 'Karuchithaivu' by Pudumaipithan, he introduces the character Sundaram Pillai thus:

> 'For him, chewing betel leaves is not a ritual. It is a meditation. A way of life.'
>
> 'In the southern direction or the direction of Yama (Death God), there is lime. He will keep it in solid form or as powder first. Then he organizes the betel leaves by removing their stems. He pastes lime into the leaves. He puts supari granules and folds the leaves. He puts it in the mouth and searches for tobacco....'

Pudumaipithan is similar to the Sundaram Pillai character he created. He used betel leaves at least twenty times a day. His friend A. Muthusivan writes, 'Pudumaipithan is crazy about betel leaves. Even when someone photographs him, he will keep the betel leaf and tobacco in the corner of his mouth. It is a ritual for him.' He chews betel leaves day in and day out. He does not have time for rest. He goes to bed late into the night. He wakes up early in the morning. After a bath and morning coffee, he takes a nap. He sleeps on his tummy like a frightened child, all folded up. For him, sleep is also a meditation. Even during the night, he will not have an uninterrupted sleep. He will wake up to chew betel leaves once and go back to bed. If someone like me is staying with him, he will take the liberty of waking me up. 'I am not getting sleep. Let us talk.' He will not mind my sleepiness. He will start the conversation and will chew the betel leaves.

I am thinking of an incident when I write about his half-sleep and quarter-sleep habits. He was writing the script for Gemini Studios. He did not even complete a quarter of the script. He did not even sit down to write. He came under tremendous pressure to showcase at least some part of the script. He and I had a conversation till 2 am one day. We went to bed after that. When I woke up around 7.30 am, Pudumaipithan was brushing his teeth near the well. I could see fifty to sixty sheets of writing on the table. Film script. Dazzled by this, I asked him what it was. He told me that he could not sleep and wrote the script. It would be a surprise for other writers to see so many pages written in such little time.

The readers may be interested in knowing the writing habits of Pudumaipithan. Sometimes, he works non-stop and delivers like crazy. There are many months when he will be like *Kumbakarna*. He will not easily touch the pen. If he wields the pen, it won't be easy for him to rest it. Some magazine representatives will get take word and advertise in the magazine about an upcoming short story from Pudumaipithan. Then they have to meet him many times before they can get the story done. Some of them make vain attempts to get a story from him. He does not want to write some sub-standard story just because he is under pressure from someone. He has great respect, value, and commitment to his writings. He will dodge as much as possible when the magazine editor tries to get a story from him. When he comes under compulsion to give the story, he will work hard to deliver it. I asked him about his delaying tactics. 'I should not make it so easy. Let them make an effort.' But I know that is not the intention. It is pure laziness. The editors will ask him, 'Have you decided upon the story? Or do you have to think about it?' Pudumaipithan responds: 'I have formed that in mind. All I have to do is to write.' He will start telling a story to the editor. The editors will leave with great confidence. The story narrated by Pudumaipithan also will disappear into thin air.

Pudumaipithan does not write stories and essays with any poise. He will write so fast that he will not stop. There is so much speed. The only break is when he chews betel leaves. His early works had several jumps, according to critics. The pace of his imagination and pen are unique. The jumps mentioned by the critics may be due to this behaviour of the writer.

His handwriting is not beautiful. It looks like a shorthand script. You see lines here and there. You have to bring the paper up close to your face tor read some Tamil words from it. Some people may not have a great destiny. But their handwriting looks beautiful. In the case of Pudumaipithan, his handwriting is worse than his destiny. You cannot easily read his story or essay. It is the worst kind of scribble, which you cannot make out. 'I understand my handwriting. The person who typesets it also understands' is Pudumaipithan's take. The translation jobs he has done under the pressure of deadlines in newsrooms may be the reason behind such messed-up handwriting. He writes with Sheaffer pens so that the pace of writing is quick. He never writes with a pencil. He does not dip the nib and write.

Some writers have to sit down and write their stories. They will not be able to dictate their stories. They feel very conscious and cannot get the words out when it comes to dictating. Pudumaipithan writes on his own. He is also able to dictate his stories to others. He will be very fast in dictating stories. I remember one such instance.

Thiruvananthapuram Chidambaram asked Pudumaipithan for a story, essay, or poem for his *Kavikkuyil* special edition. Pudumaipithan dodged as much as he could. Chidambaram will not give up. 'Please dictate. I will write it down,' said Chidambaram. Pudumaipithan reached Chidambaram's house. A plate filled with murukku, banana chips, young betel leaves, areca-nut, Jaffna tobacco, water to clean his mouth, pen, and paper awaited him. Amazed at this arrangement, Pudumaipithan was happy. Subramania Bharathiar was traveling in a horse carriage. His companion ate channa or peanuts saying, 'It tastes like nectar.' Bharathiar told the driver to accelerate the vehicle, 'Go forth.' Even a great poet like Bharathiar needed the inspiration of words from people close to him.

Pudumaipithan had a deep look at the stuff on the table. 'All the wartime materials are ready. Should I start dictating?' said Pudumaipithan.

'Sure,' said Chidambaram.

'Ok. Take the paper. Take the pen. Keep writing as I tell you,' said Pudumaipithan.

Pudumaipithan dictated. Chidambaram wrote it down. 'Song and its Path' is the title of the essay.

When it was almost done, Pudumaipithan stopped, and chewed betel leaves. He started again. But he stumbled.

'Brother! Brother! Let the essay remain there. I am getting a song. Please write it down,' said Pudumaipithan.

Under the mushroom
Cockroaches ruled
In the town of peasants
Cactus sprouted...

The song went on for about thirty lines and then faced a stumbling block.

'My stock of song is exhausted. Take the essay again,' said Pudumaipithan.

The essay was completed that day. The song was completed the next day. *Kavikkuyil* published the poem with the title 'Maha Kaviyam'.

In an essay on Pudumaipithan, the writer K. Alagirisamy says, 'He has as much respect for his works as we have.' Pudumaipithan is very involved with his stories. He treats his stories as his children. He showers love on them. He gives as much respect to it as he gives to a sacred object. It is a great quality for any writer. Some writers don't have much respect for their works. That is why they treat them so cheaply. Pudumaipithan values and respects his work. If someone criticizes it, he will listen to it. If someone diminishes it, he will respond violently to it.

I wish to mention two instances here. Pudumaipithan came to meet me in the media office where I worked. At the same time, another magazine editor had come to ask for an essay from a writer who was my colleague. On seeing Pudumaipithan, he asked him to give a story. It looked as if he was asking for a bride at a wedding function. His magazine is not of great quality. 'Appa, don't ask me for a story. Your magazine cannot stand my story. My story is like fire. It is fire. Your magazine will turn into ashes. Please know that,' said Pudumaipithan. This terrific response shows us how much value he assigned to his stories.

Two publishers had come to see Pudumaipithan. Pudumaipithan had a story with him. It was a story about Goddess Saraswati. Saraswati symbolizes truth. You cannot suppress the truth by smear campaigns. Pudumaipithan has described Goddess Saraswati as a form of purity. The idea in the story is of a higher level. Comprehension can be challenging. He read out the story to them. It shocked the publishers. When they were about to leave, they took the manuscript from Pudumaipithan. They tore apart the manuscript and discarded it. 'Why don't you write something else? Can't you get some other topic?'

Pudumaipithan got very angry. He did not express his anger.

'You have torn it apart. You have killed a child. But remember one thing. I am not a sterile person. I can give birth to a stronger child. See you later,' is how he bid them farewell. Unfortunately, he did not give birth to that stronger child after that.

Only when a person of substance criticizes his work, does Pudumaipithan pay attention to it. If someone tries to please him by saying, 'Your story is brilliant,' he rebuffs it peremptorily.

He chases such people away saying, 'To say that my work is good is nothing. Don't try to pull me down.'

Some people will pretend to be experts in literature. They would say that they have not understood some of Pudumaipithan's stories. 'This story is not meant for you,' is the typical response of Pudumaipithan to such people.

There is a misconception that Pudumaipithan has not encouraged criticism of his work. That is not a fact. He engaged with people who had genuine feedback on his work. Pudumaipithan engaged with other friends and myself, when we brought serious feedback on his works of literature.

There is another misconception about Pudumaipithan. 'He is a difficult person. It is not easy to interact with him,' is a comment from some people. They have not understood him well. People who could not stand his frankness in speech are the ones who passed such comments. Pudumaipithan interacts with all kinds of people. He does not look at the language, religion, or race, of the person. He had friends from across the spectrum. There is a set of people Pudumaipithan disliked. Hypocrites, self-promoters, copycat literary personalities, and coterie-builders are the ones he could not stand. He calls them names. He exposes those who do copycat literature. He will fight with them. Whenever he happens to meet them, he will tell them to their face what he thinks of them. He will call them by the nicknames he has given them. He will not give a damn about their responses. If someone is justifying an act of wrongdoing, he will be direct in condemning it. That is the reason some people never wanted to get closer to him.

Pudumaipithan has a compassionate mind despite his harsh criticism of hypocritical things. He is open and innocent when he interacts with people. He does not discriminate. He moves with people from all walks of life. He shows so much love and affection to his wife. He shows the same affection to a rickshaw driver. He will have nice conversations with the waiters in the hotels. He will speak in the same way to the owner of the hotel. The same warmth can be felt when he talks to the *paanwala* outside the hotel. The people who are struggling with livelihood challenges enjoy talking to Pudumaipithan. A rickshaw driver will feel free to come and ask him for money to have food. The driver asks him to compensate for the travel fare. He will oblige. A rickshaw driver from near the Royapettah tram-shed came and spoke to Pudumaipithan through the window. 'Swami, I have nothing to eat. I am hungry. Give something to eat.' He did not have anything to give that day. The driver had to go back empty-handed. The next day, Pudumaipithan and I ordered dinner from a hotel and it had sizable leftovers. He took it to the tram-shed and found the rickshaw driver and gave it to him.

Pudumaipithan treats senior writers and young writers alike. He does not discriminate between the young and old. He appreciates talent. He encourages young writers. He hates people who don't have the fire to excel in the craft. One has to come and see him as a friend. He does not like persons who claim to be his disciples or ardent fans. A friend introduced Alagirisamy to him as 'your disciple.' Pudumaipithan retorted, 'Don't say he is a disciple. Disciples don't have brains. Please say that he is a friend.' There is another instance Pudumaipithan mentioned to me. A writer has dedicated his book to Pudumaipithan and said that it is a symbol of Eklavya Bhakti. Pudumaipithan got irritated because of this. 'Eklavya? Bhakti? Who needs the *sishya* tradition? He will be sorted only when I ask his thumb as a gift,' he said.

When Pudumaipithan was in Pune, a reader, K.T. Thevar from Mumbai, wanted to see him and wrote a letter. Pudumaipithan wrote the following:

> 'I don't have any objection to your coming here and staying with me for a night. That is a pleasure.'
>
> 'I don't know about you. But that will not be a stumbling block for our new relationship or mutual familiarization. But to have an image of me as a two-headed cow, new film star, fire-eater, big man, and jet propeller plane is quite an exaggeration. I will not like it. I have a place for friends. I have space for new friends.'
>
> Yours truly,
> The one who you wish to meet,
> Cho. Vriddhachalam

Pudumaipithan welcomes friends. He goes in search of friends. My relationship with Pudumaipithan is an interesting story. I don't want to explain it here. During one of his trips to Tirunelveli, Pudumaipithan listened to my story 'Farewell' at A. Srinivasa Raghavan's home. He liked the story very much. He asked him, 'Who is this Ragunathan?' He wanted to see me. I was not in Tirunelveli then. We did not get to see each other for quite some time. In the meantime, *Dinasari* carried a harsh criticism of the debut book of an author. Pudumaipithan wrote that criticism. I wanted to write a rejoinder to that criticism. The writer who fell prey to that criticism, is a common friend of Pudumaipithan and myself. A. Srinivasa Raghavan, Thuraivan, and I discussed it, and decided that I would write a rejoinder. I sent the rejoinder to *Dinasari*. But *Dinasari* did not carry the rejoinder. The newspaper was afraid of a literary rivalry developing around such a response. Pudumaipithan had read the rejoinder. I later joined *Dinamani* in Chennai. Pudumaipithan used to visit *Dinamani*. We got to meet each other. He praised 'Farewell' and the rejoinder I wrote without knowing I was the person who wrote both the texts. When he came to know that I was the author of them, he was very happy. 'You are my type. I was looking for you,' he said, and engaged me in a conversation.

There is a reason behind narrating this instance. Pudumaipithan loves talent. Even if someone had written against him, he would love to work with them. I introduced Alagirisamy to Pudumaipithan. I told him about the 'Venthazhal Vegathu' story. He liked the story.

He asked us to bring the story. He read the story and appreciated it. He took it to *Kalaimagal* magazine and got it published.

I wrote a short story 'Vendrilan Endrapothum.' The editor of a magazine met Pudumaipithan and me in our home and discussed publishing the story. The story is long and would have required at least eleven pages. He suggested it can be published as a two-part story in his magazine. We felt that it should be published in one go. The editor said that a story of a woman writer should be carried in the edition. He insisted that my story would take two consecutive issues for complete publication. The woman writer was not writing stories of great quality. Pudumaipithan got angry. 'If you wish to publish this, please publish this in full. Or else publish that woman's story and publish multiplication tables on other pages. They are all the same.' The editor was upset. He left immediately.

Pudumaipithan is always encouraging new talents. He will do his best to support young talents. The instances I cited demonstrate this quality of Pudumaipithan.

Pudumaipithan had some of the best qualities a person can have. He also has some adverse qualities. The commitment and honesty in his writing may not be present in his speech. He appreciates some writers when they meet him. After the writer is gone, he will say nasty things about him. 'Why did you praise him?' I asked. I wanted to draw attention to this. He said that this is the best way to derail the person. But his praise is genuine. He never had any bad intentions about anyone. It was just that his speech had no restraint.

Whenever Pudumaipithan travels in a bus or a tram, he keeps the tickets and will only discard them in the dustbin when he reaches home. I asked him, 'Why do you do this?' His response was 'Why should I throw it on the streets?'

He tells lies with no purpose of deceiving someone. He does not get any benefit from these random lies. I feel he tells lies for fun. There are two examples of the lies he uttered.

Pudumaipithan's wife went to her hometown and came back. A friend asked him one day, 'Did you not bring her back?' He responded, 'I will go and bring her back.' They kept talking and reached Pudumaipithan's home. Kamalambal was there at the doorstep. 'You lied to me,' said his friend. 'Did I say that?' was the response of Pudumaipithan.

Pudumaipithan and his friend roamed the city and entered Jyoti Nilayam of A.K. Jayaraman in Triplicane, Chennai. Jayaraman understood that both of them had a long and tiring day and asked them what the matter was.

Pudumaipithan mentioned the name of a famous writer and said that he was dead. He added that he and his friend went to the crematorium and came back. It soon turned out to be a false statement.

It is strange why Pudumaipithan used such lies without any reason or benefit. Many people who know him also wonder how he got that adverse habit.

Pudumaipithan takes liberties with his best friends. He will even leave his food and have a conversation with them when they come. He will also get angry with them. Once he cools down he will be super pleasant with them. He once asked a friend for monetary help. The friend could not help him at the moment. 'You are dishonest. You don't help people who need it. You don't support your friends,' is how Pudumaipithan scolded him. The friend mobilized some money and reached Pudumaipithan's home the next day. On seeing him, Pudumaipithan apologized profusely. He asked for his forgiveness.

Pudumaipithan spends generously when he has money. He is crazy about buying books. He will visit a bookshop on salary day. If he likes a book and if it demands all his money, he will buy it. He will go hungry the next day. He will come and finish some books in one breath. He will keep some books in the bureau and forget about them. His behaviour in matters of spending is a challenge. He once bought about 100 Gillette razors at once. Is he going to sell them in retail? You will be surprised at his behaviour. He bought them because he had some extra cash with him. If he has cash in hand and sees a nice product, it is a huge challenge. He bought a toilet case for ten or fifteen rupees because it looked beautiful. He and his wife quarrelled over that. When someone comes home to collect some balance he will tell the person 'Ask her' and she will tell the person 'Ask him.' It was to settle such problems that Pudumaipithan handed over his salary to Kamalambal during his *Dinasari* employment. He would take money from her for daily expenses. It sorted out the quarrels briefly. The quarrels resumed later.

Pudumaipithan did not have the luxury of wealth throughout his career. His enthusiasm is undying whether he had money or not. Even if he was not sure about his next meal he would remain happy and speak with enthusiasm. He and I found ourselves in a financial crunch. When I got disillusioned he told me this.

> 'Rasa, you should not worry about this. As long as we remain poor, we can write without fear or favour. If we get property and luxury, we will assume false pride. You cannot do literary service after that. Now we can attack anyone. Even if they sue me, I can say I am always bankrupt.'

It is about a specific situation. He was not an advocate of penury as a precondition for imaginative capacity. He was always in favour of a luxurious life for the writers.

He may not have found luxury all his life. He remained the light of writers. He was always kind and generous to his friends. He did not see great wealth in his lifetime.

Knowledge of Music

'We know Pudumaipithan as a short story writer. We know him as a songwriter. Does he know music? He may know music.' This is a constant topic of conversation among some of his readers.

I recall an instance to demonstrate his idea of music.

Ganesha Sharma was one of the friends of Pudumaipithan. He has a very good knowledge of music. He works with a lot of musicians. Musicians have great humor in them. Ganesha Sharma loves his conversations with Pudumaipithan.

The Thiruveezhilimalai brothers, the *nagaswaram* experts, once came to Chennai. Ganesha Sharma is a good friend of theirs. He told the musicians, 'You got appreciation from the audience. I have a wise man as my friend. Nothing like it if he were to appreciate your work.' Intrigued by that comment, the musicians wanted to meet the wise man.

Ganesha Sharma brought them to Pudumaipithan's home. 'Chovi, Thiruveezhilimalai brothers wanted to play *nagaswaram* for you,' said Ganesha Sharma. Pudumaipithan said yes to them. The vidwans started playing *nagaswaram*. Pudumaipithan started chewing betel leaves. He picked up a book to read. The musicians played brilliantly for a long time. Pudumaipithan did not show any response. He kept reading the book. Ganesha Sharma emerged from another room and laughed. 'You could not engage Pudumaipithan.' Pudumaipithan realized it was all set up by Ganesha Sharma.

What is the fact? Pudumaipithan did not even know the A, B, C, and D of music. That was the reason he could not respond when the brothers played *nagaswaram*. The *nagaswaram* brothers became close friends of Pudumaipithan. Whenever the brothers came to Chennai, Pudumaipithan would go and see them. He did not go to their concerts. He asked them for a *nagaswaram* as a gift. He persisted and finally got that gift from the brothers. He once showed me that *nagaswaram*.

'What do you do with it?' I asked.

'It is to intimidate our visitors,' he said. 'If Rajaratnam Pillai is writing a column for a newspaper, can't I play *nagaswaram*?' he added.

Pudumaipithan intimidated some people with the *nagaswaram*. When some visitors overstayed, he asked them 'Do you want to listen to some *nagaswaram*?' and brought out the instrument. The visitor would be shocked. 'I wish to have a bath. If you are staying here, listen to me play the instrument.' The visitor would have no option except to leave.

Pudumaipithan did not know music. He was not interested in knowing about music. The writer Alagirisamy knows music. Pudumaipithan argued with him about music. Pudumaipithan won the argument. Algirisamy could have easily won a debate on music. Pudumaipithan diverted the argument and took control of the conversation.

Do you remember Pudumaipitan's *Baktha Kusela*?

'...the *nagaswaram* player takes Kedara Gowli raga and does the *alapana*. The band brings out the best of Rule Brittania...'

This how he describes the temple festival scene. You may wonder why he has used the name of the raga in the story. Yes. It is only a story.

Orator

You would not realize the amount of time you spent if you kept talking to Pudumaipithan. He was such a great conversationalist. But he was such a disaster as a public speaker. He treated the audience like a set of friends who had come home to have a chat while chewing betel leaves. He adopted a conversational approach while delivering public speeches.

It was 1943. When he was in Tirunelveli, the students of Hindu college invited him to give a talk. A. Srinivasa Raghavan was presiding over the meeting. After the introduction of the president, Pudumaipithan was invited to speak. As he rose to speak, the sound of applause became louder. He was not swayed by the applause. He took it easy and laughed out loud. He started speaking.

There was no introduction in the speech. There was no reverence. 'This teacher-president of yours, Ki. Ramachandran, and I, along with others, spent time in Chennai Mookar Nallamuthu street. We had betel leaves together. We discussed literature together…' he kept blabbering.

He talked to some of them from the podium. They kept quiet out of respect.

He adjusted the handcuffs of his *jippa*, scruffed his hair, took out a kerchief and tied it around the neck, and did all his gimmicks on the stage. He eventually came to talk about his stories, which was the topic set for him.

> 'They keep saying, don't write this. Don't write that. I want to ask them, what is your problem? Don't I have the freedom to write about what I want? Do I have to suppress the truth just because elders are asking me to do so? You can abort a fetus. But you cannot suppress an opinion.'

He went silent for a moment and then continued.

'No. I cannot say everything I want. That is not ok. We can birth children without responsibility. We cannot express opinion without responsibility.'

Silence again.

'I know how to be responsible. People are writing without purpose. I cannot do that,' he continued.

> 'You are reading my stories now. Tell me. How do you like them? Love stories. Bharathiar sang about the moon. He imagined it as a flame of pearl. These writers cannot write without the moon and breeze. They don't have stories without these characters.'
>
> 'In my stories, you don't find the painful dream of love. My woman protagonist will sell her chastity to feed her husband. The sex worker protagonist will lead a dignified life. She will not seek alms. No moon. No breeze. My Chempakaraman Pillai went in the dark; he came back in the dark…'

It may look incoherent. But he drove home the message.

Pudumaipithan spoke about politics once in a school in the Big Street in Triplicane, Chennai. The editor of *Kalaimagal*, Ki.Va. Jagannathan, was the President of that meeting. Very few people attended the meeting. He followed the same conversation style there as well. He forgot a name during the speech. I was sitting opposite to him. 'Rasa, you tell me.' I did not know what he was asking for. I kept quiet. 'Leave it. Some goddamn name.' He managed the situation with by adopting a satirical tone, born out of frustration.

When he was very young, he said yes to a request for a public speech. The meeting was in Palayamkottai centenary hall. The hall can accommodate nearly one thousand people. Pudumaipithan spoke to a handful of people who gathered there.

'The missing areca nut cutter' was the topic. 'Cutting wood...chopping meat...' is an old Tamil song, which he had to open with. As he went to the stage, he forgot the song. He tried to recall it. The Tamil teacher, K. Arunachala Gounder. was sitting close to the dais. He was his good friend. He asked him to help. 'I forgot the song. I forgot the meaning. Please tell me...' he pleaded to the teacher from the podium.

Such were the oratorical skills of Pudumaipithan.

Some Unforgettable Moments

There was a meeting in Chennai to honor a poet. One young writer has the habit of going to such meetings and reading a poem in praise of the author. He printed and framed a poem for this event as well. Pudumaipithan and his friends were standing in a corner of the meeting. The young writer showed Pudumaipithan the framed poem.

'Oh, a congratulatory poem! Very good,' said Pudumaipithan.

The young writer expected Pudumaipithan to comment on it. As he did not comment, the writer asked. 'How is the poem?'

In the meantime, the President of the meeting invited the speakers to the dais, and called the name of the young writer.

"They have called you. Go and recite the poem,' said Pudumaipithan. The people around enjoyed the satire in Pudumaipithan's words.

In the magazine *Kalaimagal,* the book review section is called 'Uraikal' (Benchmark). Some literary creators started talking about it. One writer wanted to know if the letter r used in the title of the section is the soft r or the hard r. Pudumaipithan, without giving it a thought, said it was the hard r. The writer who raised the doubt said, 'The word comes from the Tamil word for friction. So it is soft r.' Pudumaipithan realized his mistake. He did not cede. 'If you press r hard… you naturally get a hard r…' The Tamil language has soft r and hard r sounds. Pudumaipithan managed the embarrassing situation by explaining how he over-stressed the soft r. It was a lame excuse. The people around him understood that he made a mistake and corrected him.

Puduamipithan and I came back from a commendatory meeting. Pudumaipithan had a very low opinion of the literary creator who was the subject of the meeting. Many leaders and celebrities had commended the writer so much that Pudumaipithan felt bored.

'Rasa, I heard two women speak. Do you know what?' Pudumaipithan asked.

'Is it a story or…'

'Listen. It is a song…'

Pudumaipithan composed a poem praising the literary figure and attributed it to one of two women. The other woman now responds:

'Yes, Akka.
Pappad seller
Parvathi's aunt's daughter
Said the same thing the other day.'

I told him the grammar was not right. 'How will the *pappad* seller know grammar?' said Pudumaipithan. 'The opinions of all these people and the random pedestrian are the same. Let us go,' he added.

When we came out of a public meeting, a writer accompanied us. He is not a prolific writer. But he is very fond of liquor and women. A bookseller and his daughter were walking ahead of us. The writer asked Pudumaipithan, 'Is she his daughter?' Pudumaipithan was quick, 'Poor thing. She is quite young. His grand-daughter.'

He turned to me and said, 'I saved the girl.' He added in a hushed voice, 'Had I told him it was his daughter, he would have followed her.'

One author wrote a book about methods used in Western literary criticism. He filled the book with a lot of quotations from the books on Western literary criticism. He did not seem to have understood those concepts. A friend who wrote a foreword to the book quoted a song by Desika Vinayagam Pillai.

'You eat green grass
And provide white milk.
Will you share
That secret, Cow!'

The friend commended the author for grasping great ideas and providing insightful perspectives. Pudumaipithan read this. 'It is a bull that eats hay and excretes the same hay,' he commented.

P. Sri. Acharya was reading many commentaries of Kamba Ramayanam and writing his Chitra Ramayanam. He could not find the appropriate commentary from different commentators. Pudumaipithan entered his place at that moment.

'Cho. Vi, what is the meaning of this poem? The commentators are not clear.'

'Yes, yes. The commentators have only hidden Kambar further,' emphasized Pudumaipithan.

Our friend Mullai Muthaiya and I went to have coffee with Pudumaipithan. The idea was to have breakfast. As soon as we entered Pudumaipithan ordered coffee.

We asked him, 'Don't we have to eat?'

'Correct. Coffee first. Dosa next. Another coffee again,' said Pudumaipithan.

'What is this new habit?' I asked.

'You don't know. If you want to eat the dosa made in this shop, you have to have coffee before and after that,' explained Pudumaipithan.

Pudumaipithan and his friends went to a hotel one day.

'What is the hottest thing available?' Pudumaipithan asked the waiter.

'Idli'

'Go. Bring it.'

The waiter brought the idli. It came with a bowl of boiling sambar. Pudumaipithan broke idli into pieces. He felt the coldness of the idli. He understood the business secret of using the boiling sambar on the cold idli, to make it hot.

He called the waiter.

'What is this? The soul had gone cold.'

The waiter did not understand. 'Only the sambar is hot. The idli has already died,' explained Pudumaipithan.

A film company produced a film at a high cost. The film took a long time to complete. The company copied several elements of new English films and added them to it. Pudumaipithan commented on this. 'They are copying from many films. Do you know what it will look like in the end? It will look like the shirt of a tambourine player.'

Tambourine players in Tamil Nadu used to stitch shirts using many pieces of old clothes, because of poverty. That does not look nice from the perspective of middle-class people. Pudumaipithan meant that the film would be a disaster at the end of the day.

An editor got the support of some friends and started a publishing house. A prospectus carrying the names of all stakeholders was published. The person who invested the highest capital found his name last on the list of directors. 'The person who put the most money is finding his name at the bottom,' a friend remarked.

Pudumaipithan commented, 'He has to carry the fellows who are on top of the list. That is why he is at the bottom.'

Pudumaipithan was with *Dinamani* back then. He would read the proofs before they went for printing.

Even if he was extra careful, some composers would skip the corrections made by him. He got irritated and wrote at the end of the proof, 'God Supports Us.' The composer came and asked him if he had to print that last line as well. 'No. No. I have done my best in proofreading. If mistakes are printed, it is God who will support me. Not you. That is why I added that line,' said Pudumaipithan.

Pudumaipithan kept talking for long hours. He and his friend kept talking through the night for several hours. His friend asked, 'We go on talking. What is the time?'

'Why do you worry about it? We are Perumal who transcended time,' said Pudumaipithan.

Though Pudumaipithan called himself someone transcending time, he had a wristwatch. He wouldn't wear it on his hand. He used it only to go to work on time. He did not use it for any other purpose.

Pudumaipithan wanted a book on Panchalankurichi Kattabommu published. A publisher asked a writer to write the book and released it. The publisher gave a copy to Pudumaipithan and asked him for his opinion. Pudumaipithan read the book and commented on it by saying 'It is castrated Kattabommu.'He referred to the lack of speed in the narrative.

An author published a metaphorical story in a magazine. Another writer used the same story to write a song in the same magazine. Pudumaipithan commented on this:

> 'The husband went in search of his lover in the dark. The wife went in search of her lover in the dark. Both the husband and wife met each other in the dark and came out into the light. They blinked. The story here is similar. The story writer and the poet are from the copycat literati. They copied the same story from different sources. The story writer should not say that his story was copied. The poet also should not claim innocence. It is a fact.'

Navayuga Prasuralayam printed one of Pudumaipithan's books. Pudumaipithan sat on the pile of printed papers and smoked a cigarette. He threw the butt and it burned the printed papers. Others rushed to the spot and extinguished the fire. Pudumaipithan did not do anything to put out the fire.

'What kind of man are you? Your book is burning. You are not doing anything about it,' shouted Karaikudi Sa. Ganesan.

'Why would you put out the fire? The ashes would have made you philosophical. We wasted all that opportunity,' Pudumaipithan responded with coolness.

Pudumaipithan did not like hypocrites. A friend talks so much about communism and calls himself a communist. He has been an enthusiast of communism. But he is not a communist. He came to Pudumaipithan and said he was a communist.

Pudumaipithan did not take things lightly. 'If you are a communist, please remove your sacred thread and the namam on the forehead.' The friend felt the jolt.

'Communism asks you to erase class divide. You are not even able to erase the caste divide,' added Pudumaipithan. The friend saw the point Pudumaipithan made.

Alagirisamy, Pudumaipithan, and I, went to Tamil scholar S. Vaiyapuri Pillai's house. On the way to his house, Alagirisamy mentioned the research on Thiruvalluvar by Vaiyapuri Pillai which had been published in a Tamil magazine. Another Tamil scholar told Alagirisamy, 'Vaiyapuri Pillai is always like this. He traces the legacy of old Tamil poets, from their period to relatively modern times.' We – all three of us - had a great opinion of Vaiyapuri Pillai's research. We saw his research as quite well-balanced. We asked

Pudumaipithan for his comments on the Tamil scholar's take on Thiruvalluvar.

'Scholar! Scholars take pride in saying that our literature originated several thousand years back. Our scholars will be happy to know that, according to the theory of evolution, the first chimpanzee is a Tamil chimpanzee,' he quipped.

Pudumaipithan and Alagirisamy waited for the Route number 14 bus for a long time. It took almost half an hour to come.

'Why is it taking such a long time to come?' asked Alagirisamy.

'Oh! It is the bus that takes Raman to the jungle. It naturally takes a long time to come back,' said Pudumaipithan.

Some writers went to Pudumaipithan's home to see him. He was sitting on a mat that was torn. He took another mat that was torn and asked them to be seated. 'Please sit down. It is the Sangapalagai of writers,' he said. Sangapalagai was a forum of brilliant Tamil scholars in Madurai, during the rule of Pandyas.

Raja Ariyaratnam, the editor of *Eezhakesari*, came to Chennai. He met Pudumaipithan in Jyoti Nilayam Prasuralayam. *Prethamanithan*, a collection of translations by Pudumaipithan, had just been published by Jyoti Nilayam. Pudumaipithan gave a copy of the book to Ariyaratnam as a gift. He wrote this in the book: 'Wish to do good…but don't do it.'

Pudumaipithan went to A. Srinivasa Raghavan's house for the first time. Heavy winds cast dust on everyone. The dust fell into Pudumaipithan's eyes. He rubbed his eyes and reached the house of Srinivasa Raghavan. Srinivasa Raghavan stood rubbing his eyes to shake off the dust.

Pudumaipithan asked him who he was, to ascertain if he was Srinivasa Raghavan.

'Yes, I am. I am not sure who you are.'

'How will you know? No one can open their eyes in this dust,' said Pudumaipithan introducing himself. 'I saw you speaking at the Nellai Manavar Sangam yesterday. I have come to befriend you,' he added.

'That is why you come crying,' said A. Srinivasa Raghavan, smiling.

'You are also crying. Dust is so powerful. It does not leave anyone. If we cry when we meet, we will smile when we leave,' said Pudumaipithan.

When Mahatma Gandhi came to Chennai, there was a meeting of writers in T. Nagar. Pudumaipithan also got an invite. The organizers gave the participants badges identifying them as writers. The badges were printed in Hindi. Pudumaipithan did not know Hindi. But he knew what the Hindi alphabet looks like. He deliberately pinned the badge upside down. To whoever asked him, he said, 'It is okay to pin writing in a language that is not known to me, in any way.' 'What kind of language is this? The letters look like owls hanging upside down. That is why I flipped it. So that it looks beautiful,' was his comment.

There was a reception meeting for Marathi writer Mama Warerkar in Chennai. After the meeting, the writer Kothamangalam Subbu invited Pudumaipithan and other writers home. That was the time Subbu wrote his 'Gandhi Mahan' story. He wanted to read it to all of us. 'If you promise to give us dinner and take us to a film, we will come,' said Pudumaipithan. Subbu agreed. We all went to his house.

Subbu read out his Gandhi Mahan story. We listened to him. Pudumaipithan did not say anything. Pudumaipithan appreciated the village stories of Subbu. He could not relate to the story of 'Gandhi Mahan'.

Subbu asked Pudumaipithan, 'You are not giving your opinion?'

'I will tell you,' said Pudumaipithan. He did not say anything.

Subbu gave us *Uppuma*. Then came the pickle. Pudumaipithan does not want the pickle.

'You don't like good things,' said Subbu.

'I did not like your song. Don't think it is a good one,' said Pudumaipithan.

Pudumaipithan likes Tirunelveli Lalakadai Halwa. When I went to Tirunelveli once, I promised to send him halwa. Pudumaipithan had to go to Thiruvananthapuram a few days after I left for Tirunelveli. He asked me to meet him at the Virudhunagar railway station. He wrote the following:

You said halwa and ran away
I will catch you –
I will wait at Virudhunagar station for
The sweet delicacy.

I went to the station. He did not turn up. I sent halwa to his address through parcel post. The halwa shop owner had just joined a book publishing company as a shareholder. Pudumaipithan knew about it. He ate the halwa and wrote a letter to me.

Here are excerpts from the letter:

> '...got the halwa. I ate it today. I am afraid you may have wasted some money on it. He can go and produce books instead of making halwa. The correct consistency is missing. In Tirunelveli, halwa has the stature of a temple. We cannot compromise with it... It is because you bought the halwa, that I am forgiving it. The train only stops for two minutes in Virudhunagar. No one will object to you travelling with me to Shencottai. We can have a conversation for two hours. I will write to you once the ticket is ready. No halwa. You should come.'

Just as he wrote a poem expecting halwa at the Virudhunagar railway station, he would respond with poems sometimes.

It was the beginning of 1945.

Pudumaipithan and I don't normally share greetings during Pongal or other occasions. One Pongal, I decided to send a printed greeting card to writers and readers. Only two people responded to the card. One was the writer T.K.C. The other one was Pudumaipithan, writing under the pseudonym of Velur V. Kandasamy Kavirayar. T.K.C. appreciated my concern about false scholarships, which I had mentioned in the card. He wanted to console me by saying that it does not merit worrying about. That was a good response yet lacked imagination.

Pudumaipithan's response contained the panacea for me.

'To knock down and to attack,
To torch, we have powerful songs,
I am here; you are here; there are
Masters of the verses here.
Only when we hear the sounds of the
Masters, we can taste the songs,
Ragunatha, who is passionate about songs,
Ragunatha, don't worry!

- Velur Vena Kana

He titled this poem Pongal Hope. I also wrote a song for him.

Pudumaipithan had a principle. 'We should not mobilize funds for a writer. The writer should be able to live on his writing.' If a writer or a poet does not have enough substance to shine as a professional, he advised that they mobilize the funds as a poor person. He did not want to use the tag of a writer to seek help. We did not celebrate Pudumaipithan as a writer when he lived. During his last days, he was forced to appeal for monetary help. He should not have had to worry about taking such a step. Tamil society should feel sorry for this.

When someone would tell him that we should observe the memorial day of writers, he would say, 'Please kill the writer on a Friday. Celebrate a Guru Pooja every year.' To commend a writer is the best way to kill him, says Pudumaipithan. In his story collection *Kanchanai*, he says, 'Confining me to one stereotype is the best way to kill me.'

'We have to treat the writer as a human being. To make a hero of him is to alienate him. We should not separate him from us. We have to empathize with him and point out his errors,' said Pudumaipithan.

Have you read Pudumaipithan's story *Nasakara Kumbal* ? It was published in *Manikodi*. He wrote the first page and sent it to composition. Each page went to composition as he finished it. There was hardly any time to check continuity. This last-minute urgency is inevitable for writers.

At the beginning of the *Nasakara Kumbal* story, Maruthappa Maruthuvanar's wife Isakkiammal passed away many years ago. In the later part of the story, when Maruthappan gets hurt, his wife cries. She takes him for treatment. She converts with him to another religion.

When writers create characters, they forget the original construction and slip up like this. In this story, the wife who passed away several years ago comes alive in a later part of the story.

'In your story, people who are dead come back alive,' said a reader.

'Why should some woman die unnecessarily? I resurrected her,' was Pudumaipitan's response.

Pudumaipithan participates in the good and bad fortunes of his friends. When we interacted closely, I got a letter – a great piece of literature – from him. I worked in a newspaper. It was a capitalist institution. The rights of writers were not valued in the company. I faced a threat to my position. There was a face-off between the management and me. 'Give up your rights or leave' was the message from the management. 'You can strip me of my job. Don't strip me of my rights,' was my position. Pudumaipithan knew the issue and wrote an 18-page letter to me. I paid a fine and got the letter from the postman. He started the letter with my story. I am giving portions from the latter part of the letter here:

> '...Raghu, what am I going to tell you? Because you have the power, there is a standoff. Don't fall for hypocritical tears. Be strong. Don't be very kind here. That is just a posture. You are 22 years old now. You will be kind. I don't want to emphasize fighting for rights. I don't see the need for big words among these bad people. We don't need a Bren gun to kill a bandicoot. A log will be enough. Using a Bren gun is our ignorance. Use your strength to frighten bad elements. I am not asking you to fight for your rights. I don't believe in it. After reading your letter, I felt it may be a little too late for my communication. If you maintain the position found in the letter written to me, things will go against you. You will get opportunities if you are fired. Go and see the abattoir in Chennai. The goats come in line and the heads roll on the floor. To imagine that my Raghu is one of those goats is unbearable for me. It is a bad image. Don't play with fire again. A woman will be by your side in the future. You

> cannot keep experimenting like this then. Not everyone has the right to do experiments with truth. There will be one doing that for all of us in a story. He gives us hope. In real life, one person has done that, and made life miserable for all people around him. Two warriors are enough. Three such people won't have space to stand. I am being harsh. Don't be unsettled. I am also with you. You always have my back. Your relatives may get intimidated by your actions. I am only laughing at it. You cannot get angry with your Cho. Vi. Let bygones be bygones. Don't worry. Don't get cheated. There will not be any such situation.
>
> Yours,
>
> Cho. Vi.

I did not lose my position. I did not get cheated in the process. That is a separate story. I cited the portions here to demonstrate his emotional involvement in the well-being of his friends and his moral backbone.

Pudumaipithan took his Velur Kavirayar avatar, and wrote songs. He wrote small poems at times, just for fun. British Field Marshal Wavell suffered defeat in

Sumatra and came back during the Second World War. Pudumaipithan sang a few lines to match the situation.

'Why has the thorn fallen?
Why are Wavell's ribs broken?'
'Because they are weak.
Because they are weak.'

He wrote a fun song about another situation. A young man got close to a young woman. He had fun with her. When she insisted on marriage, he dodged. The woman became wild at this. 'It is not good behaviour. If Mother sees you and me, she will kill us. Go away,' is the burden of the song.

You did every mischief possible and today
You feel a wedding is a bitter idea
If Mother comes she will break you and put you in the oven
Run away. Get lost.

He composed songs for such situations. Sometimes, they were completed. Sometimes, they were incomplete.

Be it poetry or prose, the words are as sharp as weapons. There is a bit of satire too.

Pudumaipithan

The purpose of this book is to narrate the biography of Pudumaipithan. It is not a literary review of Pudumaipithan's works. But it will not be proper to skip past the world of his literature. I would like to write a detailed account of his literary creations as a separate work. So, I am merely summarizing the literary philosophy of Pudumaipithan here.

Pudumaipithan wrote under many names. Cho. Vriddhachalam, Cho. Vi, Velur V. Kandasamy Kavirayar, Rasamattam, Koothan, Nandi, Kabali, and Sukrachari are some of the avatars he had taken to express himself. Pudumaipithan has written short stories under these names. He has translated under these names. He has written poems and political essays; produced film scripts and plays. He has written about a hundred original short stories. He also translated about a hundred short stories. He wrote ten to fifteen lyrics. He authored many critical pieces. He has written just less than a hundred essays; a few plays; three film scripts and some novellas; along with several incomplete novels and film scripts. His works have been printed recently. Once all his works are out in print, I'll write a comprehensive literary review of them.

Though Pudumaipithan made literary contributions using many pseudonyms, the one that stayed with the people is Pudumaipithan. His short stories received critical acclaim. His genius, imaginative power, the depth of his thought found complete expression in his short stories. I will write about this later.

Tamil Nadu celebrates Pudumaipithan today as a great short story writer. When he was alive, he had more enemies than friends. His stories are not the reason for such enmity. His strong opinions earned him enemies. His reviews and criticisms were the reason for spawning such rivalry and enmity. Pudumaipithan's rigor and seriousness in reviews and criticisms earned him both supporters as well as enemies.

He would not accept arguments like 'We have to support young writers.' Even if someone is a young creative writer, we might not spot a spark in him. If you don't find the fire when the person is young, we cannot vouch for that talent. This was Pudumaipithan's position. He would not look at the age of the literary creator. He would only look at the content and talk about it. Some people feared his criticism. Some people appreciated his criticism.

Pudumaipithan wrote this in *Manikodi* magazine:

> 'The indiscriminate praising of every work in reviews, impacts the world of writing negatively. The buying of books is a new habit. If people get cheated many times, the enthusiasm for purchasing books will vanish. Critics having the mind-set of a surgeon will not kill creative talents. Bharathiar is a great example...'

Pudumaipithan acted like a surgeon while reviewing books. 'I met my bosom friend as an editor. Today, I am meeting him as an author through this book. Is it a happy thing or not? I will share this with him directly...' is how he begins a book review. He has no friends or foes when it comes to reviewing books.

Once, he reviewed a short story collection and dismissed it as a pile of trash without any authentic thought. The author met Pudumaipithan later. The author mentioned the review and told Pudumaipithan, 'You are a new kind of person. You are also crazy.' Pudumaipithan controlled his anger and said, 'Yes, I am crazy. I have not opened my third eye while reviewing your work. Had I done that, you would not be able to talk to me now.' The author left the scene in a hurry.

Pudumaipithan would write reviews in a harsh tone, as well as in a satirical tone. He once received the translation of a Hindi story, for reviewing. The translator mentioned that someone who was dejected about life and contemplated suicide, read this story, changed his mind, and became a millionaire. Pudumaipithan warned the readers that they should not expect to become millionaires after reading this story. He quoted a Tirukkural's verse 374, which talks about the nature of the world. Understanding that you can either have material wealth or intellectual wealth is important. As Tirukkal says, 'One thing to gain wealth – another to gain wisdom – The nature of the world is two.'

Pudumaipithan disliked two things in literature. 1. Plagiarized literature 2. Comparing writers and giving them titles (i.e. Bernard Shaw of Tamil Nadu, Shakespeare of Tamil Nadu).

Literary figures argued about adaptation and translation in *Manikodi* in the section called 'Yatra Margham.' Pudumaipithan is in favour of translations. He opposed all kinds of adaptations with or without due attributions. His justification is as follows:

'There is a party saying that we have to only do adaptations. They say that Tamils don't understand foreign traditions. The people who are on this side make themselves the yardsticks of literary taste and knowledge. They are asking if we have to translate Aesop's fables. The cats and monkeys in Aesop's fables don't smell of Roman culture. There is a universal language and experience. It is as common as the sky or the ocean...'

'What is the purpose of telling a foreign story? The work of a translator is the same as the work of an author doing historical fiction. In historical fiction the author moves about in time. The translator also moves in time. I am referring to the translation of contemporary fiction. The author gives life to characters that remain only in copper plates and iron or stone pillars. Then they move with the readers in real flesh and blood... Similarly, the translator also sees a human connection beyond differing attire and language.'

It is because of this strong conviction that Pudumaipithan did not accept adaptations of any kind. He mentioned it in his reviews. For instance, an author had written a play that was an adaptation. The author mentioned in the introduction that the work was for acting and not for reading. He said that it was a coffee decoction. If you added stage, scene, and actors, like milk and sugar, you will get a sweet coffee, the author added. In the review of the book, Pudumaipithan dismantled the argument in one line. 'It is not coffee; it is chicory powder.'

He attacked adaptations harshly like this. He is harsher with people who plagiarize without even calling it an adaptation. 'Some people try to contain the sun in their pockets. They call it adaptation. It is plagiarism,' he wrote. Pudumaipithan got angry when he saw plagiarism. The essays he has written under the pseudonym 'Rasamattam' are attacks on plagiarized works. The essay he wrote about the play *Bilhanan* in *Dinasari* is an example of his crusade against plagiarism. He had some harsh words for the authors of plagiarized works, saying that'[i]t is as good as claiming fatherhood for someone else's child.'

He did not like comparing Tamil authors with Western authors. He abhorred honorifics such as 'Tamil

Nadu's Maupassant' or 'Tamil Nadu's Bernard Shaw.' 'Why should we compare everything with the West? Why should we always compare the idlis of Nair shop. and the dosas of the Paramasivam Pillai hotel, with the biscuits of Huntley and Palmers?' writes Pudumaipithan in an essay. Ra. Sri. Desikan wrote a foreword for Pudumaipithan's stories. In the foreword, Desikan compared these stories with the stories of the West. Pudumaipithan did not like it. He did not like this idea of comparison.

Pudumaipithan's dislike was only towards the idea of comparison. He liked the stories of foreign authors. He spoke in a literary meeting like this: 'I am not against the love of the West. You are fond of using the toothpaste and toothbrush of the West. That is not good. Please give up the paste and brush. Please look at the opinions of the Western world.'

There was a reason for Pudumaipithan's rigorous stance in reviews. He dared to appreciate good literature. He was not dismissive of any element of literature. Why was he being harsh? He answers:

> 'Of all the books published today except those on Siddha medicine, astrology, and sex, all

> works claim some kind of literary space. It is okay to be hard on some works, in order to unsettle their claims to literary standards. If it is good literature, it will get due recognition in spite of all odds. To refer to the Indian folktale, even if many disciples of Parmartha Guru carry palm trees and do penance, the pumpkin will never become a horse egg. A reviewer should have only one quality. He should be able to recognize good works. When he sees the sub-standard ones, he should have the courage to call them out.'

Pudumaipithan's reviews do not harm. Despite several criticisms, his short stories stood the test of time.

Pudumaipithan took the avatar of Velur Ve. Kandasamy Kavirayar in 1944. He wrote songs before that as well. He assumed the pseudonym to suit the new types of songs he authored. The readers could not recognize who the new poet was. The name was new. Unlike Pithan, Siddhan, and Priyan, the sound of the name was unique. The first poem under the new pseudonym was titled 'Odatheer' (Don't run away). The magazine *Grama Oozhiyan* carried it. The writer

Ku.Pa. Rajagopalan had passed away some days before the publication of this poem. People had mobilized money to support his family after his demise. The idea of glorifying the author after his death unsettled Pudumnaipithan. Hence the poem:

After all this,
One more.
Ayya, don't mobilize money
After my death.
Don't sculpt
Your memory
Into stone
And chide it!
'The immortal one
Descended from the sky!
He disappeared
Back into the clouds!'
Don't lament like this.
I don't want this.
Leave me alone.

This is part of the song. We also glorified Pudumaipithan only after his death. We did not learn from this song of his. May this song be useful in the future. Let the idea of this song remain with us.

Some may say that this is not even a song. Is this an innovation of the literary form? Pudumaipithan initiated this new form as there was much noise over the change of forms in verses at that time. I am not going into the literary genre debate here.

The song needs rhythm and emotion. To create rhythm and emotion, rhyme and alliteration may help. But the song should move seamlessly without the conditions of rhyme and alliteration. Poetic emotion should be maintained at all costs while penning a song. Pudumaipithan adopted this technique in his composition. He gave energy to the song without distorting the rhythm. The readers will understand the form if they pay attention to the details. We cannot say this song is not successful. When Pudumaipithan wrote this, it got a very good reception. I followed the same techniques. My songs are getting a good reception. If there are difficulties in the execution of this form, we can improve the experience by constantly working on it.

Pudumaipithan used powerful vocabulary and radical opinion to infuse new blood into Tamil literature.

He used unusual words and ideas to enhance the experience of songs. These are the last lines of the song 'Unparalleled India.'

We will read the Vedas; we will measure with empty hands;
We will sell Sankarar for rice,
Above all, we talk about stories of Ahimsa
And sell Mahatma Gandhi!

It is direct and does not require a commentary!

Pudumaipithan was deeply aware of Tamil poetic traditions. You will hear rhyme and rhythm throughout his writings.

The damsels with rounded breasts
Filled with love
Are at the Blue Palace
And through its window
Lean forward,
Take the Moon and
Wear it around their waist
As a saree
And walk in style...

Yes. He took it from *Kalingathuparani*, the 12th century poem. He referred to a metaphor in the song. His talent was in recreating that image with a powerful rhythm and emotion. He used *ammanai santham*, a form of traditional Tamil poetry, in this song. He wrote in *venpas*, another form of Tamil poetry. He kept the lifeline of Tamil poetic traditions alive in his works. He sang a song on Trichy radio station:

They say it is a poem; they say it is an emotion; they say it is tradition;
They mesmerize and call it a poem – they look up
And say things that are called Tamil songs
Fool! Is this a song anymore?

Pudumaipithan introduced a new style of song-writing. He may not have perfected the form. His success and uniqueness are not in his songs but in his short stories. He succeeded in short stories and prose. Some critics may not agree with this idea. Some say he wrote in an illegible Tamil. This is an example they cite:

'The proportion of devotion for Pillaiyar depends on the amount of business one does

> with the deity. Like the zigzag temperature map of a typhoid patient. The association's support remained. So the level of devotion has not dipped yet. At 7 am, you see portable temples all around the area. The obligatory requirements of certain special items for the worship of Pillaiyar led to an increased level of bhakti among the merchants.'
>
> *('Niyayamthan,'Kanchanai)*

Those who read flippantly will not understand the message here. Satire about how devotion to God becomes business, and how ordinary mortals expect worldly gains from the deity, is explicit in these lines. This is clear and understandable. Unlike wordsmiths who write pages after pages without communicating anything, Pudumaipithan could succinctly convey messages with his extraordinary power over words.

Tamil has prose literature. It was the power of the subjects written upon that helped this prose literature thrive. It was not the power of the language. Va. Ve. Su. Iyer used words from other languages and created some magic. That was only a mild innovation. Even Bharathiar had the same technique. Some point out Bharathiar's depictions in *Gnanaratham* as an example of excellent prose. The simple, understandable style of Bharathiar is often quoted as a measure of his linguistic excellence. The use of vocabulary in Tamil prose continued to be limited until the arrival of Pudumaipithan. It was not a new outlook and imagination that helped Pudumaipithan stand out. It was the power of his language and vocabulary that made him distinct.

Here are some examples:

1. In such issues, there is no appeal against the decisions of Subbu Pillai. Most of the Azhagiya Nambiyapuram people learned the language from him. Palavesham is no exception. Even his unruly signature is thanks to the education he received from Subbu Pillai. (*Nasakara Kumbal*)
2. But he will be pushed there by the nature of his body. Energies will come together like a deluge and push the life cells to the centre. Memories will rise and die there along with the energy waves. Within the limit of time, new energies will enter his body and push him towards the earth. While descending

with new energy, his form will look at the skylines of the planets. (*Brahma Rakshas*)

3. 'A little inside is the Palace. Sculpted in stone, it showcases the majesty, valour, and dreams of Tamils. Imperial Pride is etched everywhere. The heartlessness of the Empire entices humans with its beauty. Beastly strength – courage is its euphemism – walks hand in hand with beauty. Conch and drum reverberate from inside, in unison.' (*Kanavu Pen*)
4. 'Have you seen the corner near the wall? Sex work is going on. Are you humans or animals? Your poplin shirts and shell frame spectacles came from their exploitation. Don't close your eyes like a hypocrite. They do it for their livelihood.'

(*Kavanthanum Kamanum*)

The four extracts above showcase unique voices and a language distinct from the rest of Tamil literature. The culture of Tirunelveli, the description of a body and of Brahma Rakshas's endless vision, the depiction of the Chola Empire's pride, and the bitter side of the urban underbelly are unique in the Tamil literary landscape.

Pudumaipithan added this value to the Tamil language.

My friend and writer K. Alagirisamy has written this about Pudumaipithan:

> 'In the 20th century, Bharathiar gave newness and new life to Tamil poetry. Pudumaipithan gave new life and newness to Tamil prose. Tamil had a rich poetic tradition before Bharathiar. We did not have a rich prose tradition in Tamil before Pudumaipithan. Pudumaipithan is a great asset to Tamil prose. He is the king of Tamil prose.'

Pudumaipithan's readers should pay attention to this idea of him being the king of Tamil prose. He is the king of Tamil short stories as well.

Some years ago, a person came to Pudumaipithan and said he would like to select the best twelve short stories of Tamil, and publish them in English and Hindi. The person asked Pudumaipithan to pick the best twelve stories in Tamil. He said the idea was to popularize the masters of Tamil fiction to the rest of the world. Pudumaipithan told him that if he were to pick twelve great short stories of Tamil, all the twelve stories would be his. The person got the shock of his lifetime. He conversed with him for a while, and disappeared.

Pudumaipithan's confidence may shock other writers, and even you. He was never afraid of talking about his merit in the literary sphere.

Pudumaipithan is not the only one writing stories in Tamil. Many others write in Tamil as well. Most of them are also his fans. Pudumaipithan's stories rise up like Mount Everest in comparison to the works of others. His uniqueness made him a pillar of light among the writers.

Can a writer achieve excellence only by writing short stories? This is a question that comes up often among writers. 'Pudumaipithan has written only short stories. Let us guage his genius. Let him write a novel,' said a writer-friend. He did try his hand at writing a novel. 'Annaiyitta Thee' is a novel that could not be completed by him in his lifetime.

To say that his genius is not complete because he has not written a novel is wrong. Masters such as Anton Chekhov and Guy de Maupassant expressed themselves only through short stories and excelled at it. Though both these masters have written novellas and long stories, their excellence in short stories has made them who they are today. Pudumaipithan wrote short stories, essays, and poems. His short stories brought him fame. His stories give readers a taste of the universe in which they find themselves. It is not so much about the quantity of work. It is about the quality. *Mahizhampoo,* the bullet wood tree, is small in size. It is so valuable.

A critic said this: 'Shakespeare measured the breadth of life; Dante measured its depth.' Pudumaipithan is a writer who scaled the depth of life through his works.

Each of Pudumaipithan's stories is about an issue. They are not meant to be read as a pastime. His stories posed many questions to society. They bring into focus society's scandals. The struggles of everyday life assume prominence in his narrative. He is not lost in his dreams. He tackles realism every morning.

Pudumaipithan did not cry about the everyday cruelty of life. He laughed at them. He taught the readers the same. He reported the reality of lived experiences. He may have posed questions. He did not offer hope. He did not offer answers. His storytelling is about the capacity to laugh at reality. He does not have solutions. He was angry at the suffering of people. He sulked at the injustices people endured. He could not stand the bitterness in society. He wanted to run away from reality. He remained at a distance and narrated the stories of people. Had he remained with the people and documented their stories, he could have become another Maxim Gorky. He missed that opportunity.

However, Pudumaipithan is a staunch realist. While many created an illusion and wanted people to live in a world of dreams, he took the reader to the dark recesses of reality. Parachi Maruthi goes to a tea plantation for work and returns with a firangi disease. 'You can only take away my life. Can you change anything? Can you destroy anything?' is the voice of Granny Vellaikoil towards Yama, the Lord of Death. 'Do you think I am a beggar?' is the question of a sex worker to Kavanthan. 'Sir, your handkerchief has fallen,' is the robotic voice of the waiter at the hotel. 'Appa does not know anything. Eat this. It will be sweet,' are Kandasamy Pillai's daughter's words to God. 'You have redemption for the curse. Not for sin,' are the words of Ahalya before turning into stone again. These are the words of the characters that made Pudumaipithan the king of short stories.

As far as I know, there is no short story writer who is as good as Pudumaipithan in the whole of Asia.

Who is Pudumaipithan?

Pudumaipithan is the nightmare of the copycat literati. He is a patron of authors. He has given immortality to Tamil prose. He is a genius who found a space in the Tamil literary map as soon as he arrived on the scene. The Asian *jyoti*, or light, of short stories. An inspiration for the young writers. A leader for realists. He showed Tamil Nadu how dangerous it was to make a living as a writer. He is Pudumaipithan.

My friend Manjeri Eswaran wrote the following when Pudumaipithan died:

> 'Many literary products that find currency today will become obsolete over time. Pudumaipithan's works will shine brighter then. His works are a panacea to the language. His stories dived deep into the hearts and souls of humans. They reflect the best of human intelligence and the richest achievements of human endeavour.'

True. It was not just the philanthropist Seethakathi who gave to the world even after dying. Pudumaipithan also did the same thing. His works will survive the test of time. They will never become cheap.